PRAISE FOR TRAVELERS' TALES HUMOR BOOKS

Sand in My Bra: "Ridiculous and sublime travel experiences."
—*San Francisco Chronicle* (Grand Prize Winner, NATJA)

"*Sand in My Bra* will light a fire under the behinds of, as the dedication states, 'all the women who sit at home or behind their desks bitching that they never get to go anywhere.'"
—*Publishers Weekly*

"*The Thong Also Rises* is a shoot-margarita-out-your-nose collection of travel essays stretching across the globe and into every area of embarrassment that you're thankful didn't happen to you."
—*Playgirl*

Whose Panties Are These?: "Freakin' hilarious...destructively funny stories of everything that can go wrong on the road for women, from having to buy velour panties in a very public Indian market to pondering the groundshaking question, 'Is my butt too small?' in Senegal."
—*Student Traveler Magazine*

More Sand in My Bra: "These true stories are full of bust-a-gut laughter."
—*Powell's Books*

What Color Is Your Jockstrap?: "Some stories are howlingly funny, and one, about a bot fly, will gross me out forever."
—*Goodreads*

There's No Toilet Paper on the Road Less Traveled: "Anyone who plans to travel should read this book. And then stay home."
—*Dave Barry*

Last Trout in Venice: "Traveling with Doug Lansky might result in a shortened life expectancy...but what a way to go."
—Tony Wheeler, founder of *Lonely Planet*

Not So Funny When It Happened: "Noted travel writer Tim Cahill has collected the best humorous travel pieces in one funny-bone volume."

—*Chicago Tribune*

Hyenas Laughed at Me and Now I Know Why: "Great for killing time waiting in the car."

—*Goodreads*

A Rotten Person Travels the Caribbean: "P.J. O'Rourke and Paul Theroux in a blender."

—Luis Alberto Urrea, author of *The Devil's Highway*

FICTION

Akhmed and the Atomic Matzo Balls: "This book is very sick. Highly recommended."

—J. Maarten Troost, author of *The Sex Lives of Cannibals*

Leave the Lipstick take the Iguana

Funny
travel stories
and strange
packing tips

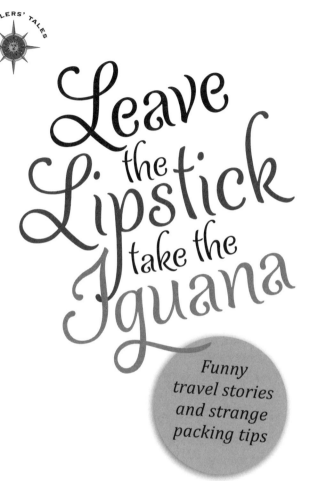

TRAVELERS' TALES

Leave the Lipstick take the Iguana

Funny travel stories and strange packing tips

Edited by Marcy Gordon

TRAVELERS' TALES
AN IMPRINT OF SOLAS HOUSE
PALO ALTO

Art direction: Kimberly Nelson Coombs
Cover design: Kimberly Nelson Coombs
Page layout and photo editing: Scribe Inc.
Interior design: Scribe Inc., using the fonts Bembo, Journal and Savoy
Author photo: Candice Caballero
Production: Natalie Baszile

ISBN 978-1-60952-053-3

First Edition
Printed in the United States

10 9 8 7 6 5 4 3 2 1

To Mom for instilling in me the love of travel and to Dad for showing me life is best viewed through the prism of wit and humor

Table of Contents

Introduction   xiii

The Horse Whisperess   1
LAURA DEUTSCH
  USA

Appendix Over and Out   7
KRISTY LEISSLE
  Ghana

I Had a Passion for the Christ   17
MELANIE HAMLETT
  Florida

Giving Dad the Bird   27
LORI ROBINSON
  South Africa/Botswana

Easter Island and the Chilean with
the Brazilian   34
KIRSTEN KOZA
  Easter Island

Why You Worry?   38
KATHLEEN MILLER
  Brazil

Thunda Chicken Blong Jesus Christ   54
AMANDA TURNER
  Vanuatu

Motorcycle Mama   62
  LEIGH NANNINI
    Greece

An Indian Wedding Nothing Like
the Movies   66
  NICO CRISAFULLI
    India

Ciao Bella   72
  CHRISTINA AMMON
    Italy

Any Bears Around Today?   76
  KIM MANCE
    Canada

Packaged in Puerto   80
  LAUREN QUINN
    Mexico

Turkish Foreplay   86
  CHERYN FLANAGAN
    Turkey

Monkeying around in Paris   92
  DAVID FARLEY
    France

Going to the Dogs with My Mother   96
  SUZANNE LaFETRA
    Minnesota

The Spice is Right   102
  MEGAN RICE
    Mexico

Drug Money 106
KATIE EIGEL
Amsterdam

Karma at the Colombo Airport 113
JESSICA LANGLOIS
Sri Lanka

Hollywood Fiction 116
TROY RODRIGUES
USA

Naked with a Passport 122
ALLISON J. STEIN
Germany

The Nakuru Scam 128
SYLVIE DOWNES
Kenya

Embedded in the Boot 132
JENNIFER MASSONI
Italy

Advice for Closet Cougars 140
JILL PARIS
France

Mt. Fuji in a Trash Bag 144
SARAH KATIN
Japan

Flashed in Fallouja 151
KELLY HAYES-RAITT
Iraq

Ditching First Impressions   154
    KIMBERLEY LOVATO
        France

Safari Sickness   161
    JULIAN WORKER
        Nepal

Meeting Mosquito   165
    JOSEY MILLER
        Brazil

Wasted in Margaritaville   171
    JILL K. ROBINSON
        Mexico

Cabin Pressure   176
    DIANE LETULLE
        France

Sometimes a Language Barrier Isn't   182
    SPUD HILTON
        Tunisia

Pricier than Prada   186
    PEGGY EXTON JAFFE
        Italy

Thank the Good Lord for Duct Tape   192
    BREGE SHINN
        Prague

Acknowledgments   199

Introduction

TRAVEL STARTS WITH AN EMPTY BAG. BEFORE WE ARRIVE AT our destination, we give thought to what we should bring or leave behind. We all have our weird preferences when it comes to packing our necessities and travel talismans. For some it's a lucky hat, a fresh journal or, in the case of one friend, a stuffed plush toy (a Japanese cartoon character named Domokun) that she poses and takes pictures of in front of landmarks around the world.

As a kid it was ingrained into me to always travel with crackers, chewing gum and tissues. When I was sent off flying solo at nine years old to New York, my mother handed me a small bag with Dentyne gum, Kleenex, and those orange-color Lance Toastchee peanut butter crackers.

For years I followed my mother's advice and carried crackers out of loyalty to the family tradition. Then one day, I stopped. I didn't tell my mom. I felt I had betrayed her by abandoning crackers, but it allowed me to explore new snack vistas. Crackers are not practical for long-distance travel, unless of course you are the type who enjoys snorting pulverized dust out of a cellophane sleeve. Instead, I began to bring crush-proof snacks, like cans of Pringles and mini M&Ms in little plastic tubes. But I could barely make it past the pre-boarding announcement without opening the Pringles and eating the entire can. Then once on board, I'd have to break open the M&Ms to counteract all the salt ingested from the Pringles. If the need for emergency food ever did arrive, my supply would be depleted before the plane ever left the gate. I realized an emergency food supply should be just that, something for an emergency—not tasty, but sturdy.

Magazines, newspapers and, especially, travel websites are always offering up advice on packing by "experienced travelers." But the articles about people who smuggle live animals taped to their body intrigue me. Creatures, like budgies, snakes, monkeys, spiders, hamsters and, yes, iguanas. Who better to give packing tips than someone who can fly eight hours with a python in their pants or a baby lemur in their bra? I can't imagine getting by security with a corkscrew, much less a seal pup in my parka.

Our baggage usually contains material items to make our journey more comfortable, or safer, or in some cases less lonely. But the real travel essentials are stories—the tales we bring with us, and the stories we take back home.

When I was twelve I went on a whirlwind tour of Europe with my parents. At a tiny hotel in Genoa, Italy, we found a violin had been left behind in the room. My dad took it down to the front desk where by some massive misunderstanding he thought they wanted him to play it. So he took the thing out of its case and gave it a go. As he was coaxing the most God-awful and torturous sounds from the instrument, the actual owner of the violin walked in to see if it had turned up. Oops.

We took that story home with us and laughed about the incident for years. It became part of our canon of travel experiences. But as I got older I began to wonder about the story the violin owner might have told his friends and family: "...and then I walked in and saw this crazy Americano playing *my* violin!"

More recently, while waiting for a flight home from Croatia with some fellow travel writers, I told the story of how I once took a lengthy entrance exam as part of an apprenticeship program in the film industry. One section of the test had a list of everyday objects such as a hairbrush, a brick, a tea cup, and a 3x5 card—and asked for five alternative uses for each item other than its intended purpose.

Under *Name 5 alternative uses for a brick,* I wrote down: paperweight, pestle, doorstop, hammer and weapon. For the 3x5 card I listed: shim, blotter, ruler, funnel and weapon. On hairbrush I came up with a backscratcher, strainer or colander, foot massager, soil aerator and, once again, a weapon. Somehow I'd latched on to the idea that, in the right hands, anything could be used as a weapon.

At the gate we were called together as a group and asked several security questions. Had anyone approached us to carry anything on the plane? Where were we going? Where had we been? What was the reason for our trip? Then the agent said: "Is there anything in your bag that looks like a weapon or could be used as a weapon?" I stole a quick glance at my friends and saw they each had identical purse-lipped cat-who-ate-the-canary looks. *Oh please don't let them start laughing,* I thought to myself. Or worse, offer up that I'd passed a test by describing objects as inherently dangerous. The airline employee looked directly at me, awaiting an answer. I wanted to reply that EVERYTHING in my bag could be deadly. But I thought better of it and said no. "Nothing weapon-like in my bag."

The most dangerous thing I had was my story.

In this collection you'll find stories of regret for things packed, such as Jill Paris and her red push-up bra, or Suzanne LaFetra with too much arctic clothing, and in the case of Kristy Leissle, a first-aid kit without enough bandages. There are also stories about letting go of mental and emotional baggage, such Laura Deutsch's corporate mask, Kimberley Lovato's sense of propriety, Josey Miller's fear of heights or Lori Robinson's rigid relationship to her father. And then we have stories of things that were left behind but might have come in handy, as in Nico Crisafulli's sobriety, Jill Robinson's morals, and Katie Eigel's guilty conscience, which luckily reappears in the nick of time.

These stories were selected not only for their comedic value, but also for how they provide a deeper examination of the human condition when parsed with wit, intelligence and hilarity. Each story reminds us that the most essential thing to bring when you travel is a wash-and-wear sense of humor. In the words of Karl Malden: "Don't leave home without it!"

Next time you pack I invite you to lighten up, let go of unnecessary baggage and, most of all, disregard conventional wisdom and advice. I encourage you to *leave* the lipstick and *take* the iguana. It might make things more interesting and I can't wait to hear about it.

MARCY GORDON
Sebastopol, California

LAURA DEUTSCH

The Horse Whisperess

*A frazzled lawyer discovers the business
end of horsemanship.*

HERE IN MARIN COUNTY, HOME TO THE HOT TUB AND PEA-
cock feather, I thought I knew the alphabet of self-realiza-
tion, abs to Zen. But I would have to travel to the base of
the Santa Catalina Mountains to become enlightened by
the Equine Experience.

My gears were grinding in overdrive from my work as
a law firm marketing consultant. Desperate for a tune-up,
I dialed 1-800-SPAFINDER.

When I explained my situation, the spa specialist didn't
hesitate. "Miraval. They cater to people like you." She
moved on before I could ask what she meant. "And they
offer a fantastic workshop, where you attain enlighten-
ment by grooming a horse."

I laughed.

"Don't laugh." She sounded offended. "It's profound.
You learn a lot about yourself."

With a Ph.D. from the Woody Allen School of Obses-
sive Introspection, I was skeptical. My psyche has been

plowed, fertilized and tilled, and I hoped there wasn't too much more to unearth. But this travel agent, whom I imagined in a warren of cubicles at some isolated outpost with an 800 number, had passion for her horse experience. I was intrigued.

Six months later, I ended up at Miraval, less than an hour from Tucson. My plan was to sleep, do yoga, and get a massage every day. Practicing mindfulness on vacation, once I arrive at mindlessness, I figure I'm there.

As a former lawyer, cross-examining other guests on activities they'd enjoyed to date came as second nature. Workaholic lawyers from New York gave two thumbs down to workshops where they were told to write about their work, then make believe they *were* their work.

"Are you from New York or California?" one asked. "California? You'll like it."

But even the most corporate, Ivy League, untherapized among them touted the Equine Experience.

It sounded simple. First you groom a horse. Then you get it to walk, trot, and canter, using nonverbal cues. Thinking I should do something beyond the vege, I signed up.

There were just two of us, me and Val, a buoyant real estate broker. Wyatt, the therapist cowboy, would shepherd us through the experience.

We sat on bales of hay and got some basic facts. To the horse, you are a predator. But the horse is more powerful than you are. Horses don't understand words including "whoa" and "giddyap." They do understand body language. They pick up on threats and fear, and they will react.

Moving into the ring, Wyatt demonstrated how to groom Monsoon, a two-story ton of horse with a ticklish spot. He taught us how to approach the horse and where to touch him to establish rapport.

The first task was to clean Monsoon's hooves. When Wyatt pinched the tendons of Monsoon's foreleg, the horse raised his hoof and dropped it into the cowboy's hand. Sometimes. Wyatt cupped the hoof in his hand and cleaned out the dry, caked mud with a sharp hook. On to the next hoof. Then, Lordy Lordy, he turned the horse around to get to the other side, by placing the side of his rib cage against Monsoon's. Keeping a hand on the horse's back, he walked around Monsoon's rump, never losing contact.

When a horse feels fear, I've been told, it may kick out its hind legs and run. A comforting thought as I imagined sashaying around the beast.

Then Wyatt curried and buffed Monsoon, brushed his face, combed his black forelock, mane and tail. Piece of cake.

Suddenly Val's elbow was piercing my ribs, her eyes riveted to the vicinity between Monsoon's rear legs.

Wyatt was on top of things. "What do you notice?" he asked. Briefed by yesterday's participants, I went to the head of the class.

"His male organ is extended."

We learned this is a good thing.

"That means he's relaxed," Wyatt commented. *Very* relaxed, I thought. And not Jewish.

Wyatt anticipated our every thought. "Don't worry, he won't urinate on you." Well, almost every thought.

"Okay, choose your horses," he said. "Who wants Monsoon?" Neither of us moved.

"What about Si Si?" he asked, indicating a horse half Monsoon's size, a speckled gray. I paused.

"Maybe you don't feel affinity for either horse," suggested Wyatt.

Yeah, right. I don't feel affinity for a horse named Monsoon who's two stories high, has a ticklish spot you'd better avoid, won't lift his hoof even for the master horseman, and when he's groomed elongates his gelded organ so fully you could use it to measure hectares.

Val volunteered to take Si Si. I was led back to the barn.

I chose a brown gelding, an Arabian beauty, tall, dark and handsome, reaffirming the wisdom that women are attracted to animals who look like them.

His name was Adieu. Perfect, given my state of relationships.

Time to groom. Now picture this. I'm standing in the middle of the ring, afraid to get near the horse. I'm a successful business owner, a mature executive at the top of my field, and I begin to cry. Fearful he'll kick me in the face or pick up his hoof and slam it into my delicate hands.

"What's your fear level on a scale of one to ten?" asked Wyatt.

"Six," I said. Liar, liar.

"What's it about?" Power, authority, the obvious answers. The people who kick you in the face, metaphorically. I couldn't admit I knew it would ruin my manicure.

"That's good," said Wyatt. "He knows you're afraid; now he doesn't feel threatened. Back up and approach again. With confidence."

I backed up, approached, retreated. Three times: marched forward, touched Adieu's shoulder, pinched his foreleg, ran away. If there had been a larger group that day, watching, I might have maintained my composure, kept the armor on. But there was relief in letting a four-legged, non-English speaker trigger a release of fear and stress deeply buried under archaeological layers of business success.

Finally, I got the hoof in my hand. Now I was afraid I was going to hurt the horse. I imagined soft little doggy paws, as I prepared to dig in the sharp hook.

Wyatt took the hoof and dug deep, fast, and hard. Thwack, whomp. I stood amazed. "It's as hard as ram's horn," he told me.

I cleaned two hooves, turned the rump around, and cleaned the other two. When Adieu tried to pull his hoof away, Wyatt showed me how to pull it back. Apparently a horse responds to boundaries. What a concept.

Then I curried, buffed and combed, now totally in love with this beautiful, cooperative horse.

As Wyatt led Adieu to another ring, Val confessed she was jealous that I could cry. Her fear, she allowed, was a nine out of ten.

Adieu was free to run. "When you meet a new horse, observe. Let it run out pent-up energy first," Wyatt advised. A good policy beyond the horse.

He showed us how to move Adieu around the rim of the arena. Standing 45 degrees behind the horse, Wyatt's body faced the animal squarely. The horse was motionless until Wyatt started to walk. Adieu picked up his pace as Wyatt picked up his, occasionally flicking the whip behind the horse, but not touching him. Through body movement he got the horse to walk, trot, canter, and stop. He showed us how to turn the horse around by repositioning ourselves.

Val did it. I did it. There was a certain thrill, though I was still skeptical, believing that the horse was trained, merely going through his paces. "If you think that, take a breath and pause," said Wyatt. I did. Adieu stopped. "Now make him canter." I sped up my pace and Adieu responded.

I felt powerful, though Wyatt was quick to point out that the horse could pulverize me if he chose to.

Back on the bales of hay, Wyatt described the typical response of corporate types who do this for team building. Some root for their colleagues to succeed. Some hope that they will fail. The most common fear of CEOs is that their covers will be blown. Underlings will see that they are shams, Wizards of Oz who have tricked others into thinking they are competent, powerful human beings.

At the spa that night, I soaked in the hot tub with the workaholic lawyers from New York.

"What did you learn?" one asked.

"Horse sense," I replied. Reminders important for work and love. That how you hold and use your body communicates more than words. Pick up on the energy. Boundaries are appreciated. An animal that doesn't speak can express more affection than many humans. When you want to get someone big and powerful turned around, put your rib cage against his and walk slowly around his rump.

Laura Deutsch's personal essays, features and travel adventures have entertained readers of the Los Angeles Times, San Francisco *magazine,* More *magazine,* Psychology Today, *and many other publications. Her essay on surviving Tuscany appeared in* Best Women's Travel Writing 2011, *and her piece on surviving a hip New York hotel was anthologized in* I Should Have Stayed Home. *Laura's book,* Writing From the Senses, *will soon be published by Shambhala, and she is currently writing an irreverent memoir about her spiritual journey around the world. Laura leads writing retreats from Tassajara to Tuscany. For more information, visit her web site at www.lauradeutsch.com.*

Appendix Over and Out

*BYOB in Ghana means something different—
bring your own bandages.*

"'Loh ma, howryoo?" I chewed noisily into the phone.

"What are you eating?" my mother demanded.

I swallowed. "A chocolate bar."

"Are you sure you should be eating chocolate right now? Did they say that was O.K.?"

"Mom, they just gave me a fish head for dinner. It still had the eyeballs in it."

"Oh my God." There was a pause, and then, "Nadia, they made her eat a fish head!"

I heard Nadia reply at a volume of one desk away, "Oh my gawd, a fish head?" I imagined them both shaking their heads at my latest disgusting misfortune. My mother's voice returned to the phone.

"Well, I guess you're O.K. with the chocolate, then."

Actually I wasn't, because it was one of those crappy Malaysian bars—a waxy brown sheen over a wafer that might have been made from compressed newspaper. But as my only alternative to this was fish head, I could hardly afford to be choosy. I looked down at my half-eaten dinner. An eyeball, complete but cooked, gazed blindly back.

I was, at that moment, convalescing from emergency surgery in Korle-Bu Teaching Hospital in Accra. Three days before, I had been traveling to Kumasi, the city in Ghana's Ashanti region where I kept an apartment during fieldwork, when a frightening illness struck.

Having finished up some research in the chocolate factories along the coast, I bought a bus ticket to return to Kumasi from Accra. With a little time to spare before boarding, I wolfed down a burrito and chocolate milkshake at Champs Sports Bar, the only place where I could get Mexican food in Ghana. So when the nausea first hit, somewhere on the outskirts of the capital, I assumed I was simply paying the price for my hasty, mismatched dinner.

But by the time we got to the rest stop halfway to Kumasi, I could no longer stand fully upright, and the other passengers were shooting me worried looks as I tried to walk around, bent over double. It felt as if a thick, immovable lump of lead had dropped into the pit of my stomach. When at last I climbed into my bed, well after midnight, the inexplicable, heavy pain kept me up through the night, as my resident gecko peered down from the wall above, nervous and twitchy. When morning dawned, I knew I needed to find a doctor.

I dragged myself outside to mime a request to my landlady's niece, who spoke only Twi, to fetch a taxi. She ran off down the dirt road and arrived back fifteen minutes later with a dilapidated cab. A complicated transaction then ensued, during which I gave the driver, who also spoke no English, vague, second-hand directions to a clinic I had heard of, but never visited, and negotiated a price. We drove for half an hour over pitted, potholed roads, through the choking exhaust of Kumasi morning traffic, searching for the clinic.

By the time I paid the up-front admission fee and settled into an examining room, the leaden ball had migrated from the center of my stomach to the lower right side. Pressing gently on my abdomen, a stately Ghanaian doctor declared that the problem might well be with my appendix, but that it would take at least four hours for a surgeon to arrive from Kumasi's public hospital, Komfo Anokye, and confirm his diagnosis. Upon receiving this news, I threw as much of a tantrum as the pain would allow, which had the happy result of halving the time it took for the surgeon to arrive, but the unfortunate one of terminating my good relations with the first doctor forever.

"I'm not waiting four hours for the surgeon to get here!" I half gasped, half shouted. "If it is my appendix, it could burst before then!"

"Are you a qualified medical doctor?" he demanded.

"No, but I don't need to be a doctor to know my appendix could burst," I insisted. "Everybody knows that." The doctor turned without a word and stalked out of the room. He refused to communicate with me from then on except through the nurses, who deposited me into a wheelchair and wheeled me to another wing, where I was ordered to lay in bed and not move.

A small but formidable nurse army formed at the foot of my bed, commanding me to swallow an array of pills, from antibiotics to Valium. I refused. We engaged in a battle of wills over the IV drip, which I eventually lost; I lay there, eyeing the thin spoke of metal poking into my vein, hoping it had been sterilized.

With no choice but to wait for the surgeon to arrive, I grasped at the positives. By Kumasi standards, at least, the clinic wasn't the worst. It seemed reasonably clean, and had some supplies. I had already seen a vision of hell in Ghana's public health system, when I took my friend Kirti to Komfo Anokye one night when he had trouble breathing. As Kirti was treated with oxygen and a battery of drugs, I stood outside his room, aghast at the sight of the hospital's apocalyptic corridors, lined with inert bodies on stretchers.

And Kirti was one of the lucky ones—he actually made it into a hospital, and could afford to pay for treatment once he got there. From my fieldwork in the cocoa-growing regions, I knew that access to health care was extremely limited for many Ghanaians, with most rural areas unserved by even a clinic. One heavily pregnant cocoa farmer had told me that when she went into labor, she would have to walk or be carried to the next village to find a midwife. This was not at all unusual.

The inaccessibility of reputable care meant that a shadow market flourished for dubious longevity aids. I'd seen salesmen board tro-tro vans as they slowly filled with passengers and give half-hour long, live infomercials about the amazing effects of the medication they were peddling, usually on behalf of a Western drug firm. Unencumbered by labeling laws, companies promoted pharmaceuticals that claimed to improve memory, delay old age, enhance eyesight, or boost mental capacity. Of course, they did nothing of the kind.

Ghana was also littered with drugs that were outright dangerous, nothing more than a random mix of chemicals in a bottle. I met another farmer who distributed reliable, over-the-counter medicines to her village. As we sat around her kerosene lantern one evening, she explained why she had taken up this side business. It made her money, to be sure, but it was also because she had lost too many friends and relatives to quack treatments. She told me about her brother-in-law, who had purchased a tonic at the local market to treat a stomach ailment. On the third day after buying it, he died. It wasn't the stomach ailment that killed him, but the tonic.

In comparison, I was fortunate to be in a clinic, with true medical professionals at hand. Nevertheless, the surly treatment I'd received from doctor and nurses alike had made me uncomfortable, and there did not seem to be any official operating theatre. If it came to it, I did not think that the clinic was an ideal place to undergo the first surgery of my life.

After two hours with such morbid thoughts for my only company, the surgeon arrived from Komfo Anokye. He ordered an ultrasound, which, to my despair, confirmed that my appendix was grossly inflamed and needed to be removed at once. He would have to operate immediately.

True panic set in. Until that moment, though I knew that I was likely having an appendicitis attack, I had been able to keep the idea of surgery at bay, within the hazy realm of possibility. When that haze solidified into cold fact—that this man was going to sedate me and cut open my abdomen, and that not one friend or family member in the whole world even knew I was ill—I finally crumpled, and wept. My mind rebelled against the thought of permitting the doctor to perform the surgery in that questionable clinic, while inside my body, my appendix was on the brink of spilling forth poison. Not trusting myself to make any rational decision, I dried my eyes, and did the thing I had been dreading: I called my mother.

Upon hearing that her daughter was facing emergency "roadside surgery" (as she called it) in the middle of Africa, my mother calmly took control of the situation from New York. She conferenced me in with a firm that exists to aid Americans in distress overseas, and I spoke to one of their doctors. After reviewing her information on Ghana, this woman said, "Do not under any circumstances have this operation in Kumasi. Get yourself to Accra immediately."

And so the decision was made. Armed with only a pain-killer and repeated silent entreaties to my appendix not to burst, I paid my bill, rushed home in another dilapidated taxi, packed a bag, and sped to the airport to catch the day's last flight to Accra. I steeled myself for the journey, wondering if the plane might do me in before my appendix even got the chance.

Although friends in Ghana regularly took the short flight, I had believed that nothing could ever induce me to board that rickety propeller plane and take off from that airport, where the "cafeteria" consisted of an ample woman stirring a cauldron of beans in a dirt yard, and rusting planes littered the sides of the runway. But I could not risk another eight-hour bus ride. I staggered into the terminal and was greeted by the pilot, a jovial Korean man. He looked at me, bent over double and sporting a large backpack, and asked why I was traveling to the capital.

"Oh, I'm having an emergency appendectomy," I replied, trying to sound casual and not stricken. The baggage screener paused mid-X-ray as the pilot whisked my pack off the belt and carried it onto the plane himself. I boarded as the propellers spluttered to life, and we rose shakily off the runway, the tiny plane lurching sickeningly from side to side. I stared fixedly out the window as we flew high above Kumasi, making odd, detached observations to the guy sitting next to me. Part of me registered how delusional I sounded, but I could not stop myself from trying to make conversation, struggling towards normalcy.

"How green it is in Ghana," I blurted out, as we teetered southward over the rainforest. The man ignored me.

"Oh, look, there's the lake where the souls of dead Ashanti people go!" He stared at his briefcase.

I swam in and out of panic, praying continually that my appendix would remain intact for just a short while longer. Forty-five nerve-wracking minutes later, we landed in Accra, the city I had left less than twenty-four hours before. An ambulance was waiting for me on the tarmac. The other passengers gawked as I was whisked away, sirens wailing, to Korle-Bu.

Once there, I was carted off immediately to the operating theatre, where I greeted the friendly surgeon and anesthesiologist as if they were the only people I had ever loved. They chatted breezily about all the things that would happen during the surgery—"And then we'll paralyze you and shove a tube down your throat to breathe artificially!"—and were soon ready to administer the anesthesia. As they did, I blurted out a desire to see my appendix after they took it out, as if this was some kind of desperate, dying wish.

I awoke to a view of a ceiling. "Where am I?" I slurred. The operating staff laughed, and one of them explained gently why I was there. She brought my appendix over for me to see, in accordance with my maniacal, last-breath entreaty. I glanced at the offending vestige, lying in a green Tupperware container. Then I fell asleep.

I soon settled into my new, appendix-less life. On the first day after my surgery, I enjoyed a steady stream of visitors, none of whom I had ever met before and only few of who displayed any meaningful medical credentials. One guy walked into my room, greeted me, flushed my empty toilet, said goodbye, and walked out. A second man came in and silently mopped half the floor, followed by a third who mopped the other half. Towards afternoon, two brand new people turned up and asked if they could pray with me. Sure, why not? I thought, and invited them in.

The man and woman took up positions at either end of my bed. They didn't ask why I was in hospital, only if I had accepted Jesus into my heart. I replied vaguely that I had been raised Catholic and they nodded, seemingly satisfied with my relationship with Jesus. They assured me that whatever had brought me into Korle-Bu was part of God's larger mystery. The man then said some energetic prayers for his own personal well being, while the woman belched repeatedly and impressively at the foot of my bed. Then they left.

The traveling prayer pair was followed by a whole bunch of people who opened the door just to ask where I was from and if I was married. I began to have the feeling they didn't receive too many foreign patients at Korle-Bu.

At first, nurses maintained a pretense that Korle-Bu was equipped to satisfy all my peculiarly American, post-operative needs. A woman appeared in my doorway on the first evening that I was allowed to eat.

"Madam Kristy," she began politely, "What would you like for dinner?"

"Thank you, I would love a glass of juice."

"There is no juice," she said, shaking her head.

"No juice?" I replied, incredulous.

"No, madam, I am sorry."

No juice? How could a hospital not have juice? What were they planning to serve me, if not juice? Schnapps? I giggled at the thought. That's what people always gave me on important occasions in the bush. As the nurse stood there expectantly, however, it occurred to me that she might actually try to give me schnapps. I decided to abandon the drinks portion altogether.

"All right, forget the juice. Have you got any vegetable broth?" The nurse went away, returning almost instantly.

"No, I am sorry, madam. There is no soup. They can't get it for you."

I gave up. "Well, just bring me whatever you have, then." Moments later, my dinner of fish head arrived, on a bed of rice. Feeling starved after days of being fed through a glucose drip, I actually picked at the fish head. It was extremely spicy.

During the day I lurched around, marveling at what appeared to be a pre-colonial paint job and gargantuan cockroaches scurrying along the floor. There were no supplies. And not just luxuries like juice—I'm talking basic supplies. There was no drinkable water, or toilet paper. One day, my bathroom ran out of toilet paper and they had to send someone out to buy a single roll. For water, I had to stagger outside to the pharmacy and purchase bottles of it myself.

My surgeon had insisted on leaving my incision uncovered, explaining that this allowed the wound to breathe and dry and heal. Several days later, my uncovered wound became infected in the peeling, grimy corridors. I visited the nurses' station to ask for a bandage. "Sorry," the head nurse replied, "we gave out the last bandage yesterday." I carried on outside to the pharmacy.

"Hello. Do you have any bandages?" I inquired of the pharmacist.

"No, I am sorry. Did you ask at the nurses' station?"

"Yes, I did. They're out."

"I am sorry."

"Do you have any plasters?"

"No, we don't."

No plasters. No bandages. Back in Kumasi, I had dragged out my first aid kit, which was so extensive I could probably have performed the appendectomy on myself in my own home, trying to decide if I should take anything from it with me to Korle-Bu. I had stopped, in my drugged haze, to remind myself that I was on my way to a hospital. They will have these things there, I thought. Funny, though, because they didn't.

Days passed, and it became clear that my uncovered wound really did need attention. I returned to the nurses' station, where a formidable woman scraped off the scab that was trying to form through the pus, and then walked out. She returned with the attending physician, who declared it was necessary to remove the stitches immediately. Chatting animatedly, the nurse cut out the stitches and swabbed my incision, then took out a precious bandage.

At that instant, an enormous cockroach—one of the African flying variety, and the size of my cell phone— scuttled across the white counter, heading straight for the sterilized instruments. I opened my mouth to sound the alarm, but the nurse had already spotted the wretched thing. She moved towards the counter, and raised her hand—the hand holding my bandage.

Impossible. I looked on in mute horror, unable to utter a syllable of protest.

As I watched, the nurse swiftly brought her hand down onto the countertop—BANG!—killing the cockroach in a well-practiced motion. Hard wings crunched into the thick body, flattened across the countertop. Briskly, the nurse swept the remains into a trashcan, and then calmly finished unwrapping the bandage. She reached down and firmly taped the bandage into place on my abdomen, covering my infected wound.

Perfectly unconcerned by this series of events, the nurse met the wild look in my eyes.

"Those cockroaches," she remarked, "they are so troublesome."

★

Kristy Leissle is a writer, professor, sailor, and long-time global voyager. She is happiest when writing about her adventures while having them, pen bent toward battered notebook while life's extraordinary moments unfold.

I Had a Passion for the Christ

She wasn't a Jesus freak until she freaked for Jesus.

AS FIFTY OTHER TOURISTS AND I ENTERED THE CAVE, A MAN dressed in a pharaoh's outfit handed us each a cracker and a teeny-tiny wooden cup of grape juice, which looked like a shot glass from biblical times. It was The Last Supper and we'd be breaking bread with Jesus himself in T-minus five minutes.

I wasn't Christian and I didn't believe in Jesus anymore, but I thought it might be kind of fun to visit the Christian-themed amusement park in Orlando, Florida. One of my favorite things to do is immerse myself in a culture that I usually make fun of in order to understand it better. I figured spending the day with Bible thumpers at a Jesus amusement park might help me see religious folks in a new light.

After exploring Noah's Ark, which had nothing but a cardboard cut-out of Jesus and an arcade game, I took a stroll through a giant plastic purple whale, where I found my man, Jonah, floating around. I tried to show off my vocals at "Celebrate Jesus Karaoke," but people didn't respond well to my performance of the only non-gospel tune in the book, "I Believe I Can Fly." I even endured a frighteningly patriotic show, the only one at Holy Land not based on a Bible story, called "The God Bless America Show," and applauded along with the crowd as the man in uniform on stage proudly announced he didn't mind being crippled for the rest of his life because getting shot in war was God's will for him.

At first it felt disrespectful being a non-believer among all these good Christian men and women, like a Russian spy wandering around the Pentagon. But then it occurred to me I'd always felt this way. Even as a kid I thought Jesus was a load of crap. Sure, I'd attended Sunday school, prayed a lot, and sung in the church choir through my sophomore year in high school, but only to make my mom happy.

As soon as I hit sixteen, though, I decided to do what I darn well pleased, mostly drugs. While all my peers spent Sunday mornings studying the Bible in church, I was always hot-boxing a joint in the parking lot or rummaging through the church kitchen with a bad case of the munchies. My mom finally dropped her good-Christian-daughter-agenda after I was busted drinking and smoking on a choir tour and sent home in a van two days early. Here I was though, a non-believer standing in a cave elbow to elbow with a crowd of Gentiles.

Once the disciple guy finished his little speech, Jesus entered the stage, cave left. I'd expected him to be the typical, distorted white version of Jesus from my childhood, or maybe even the Mel Gibson version from that terrible movie about torturing Jesus. But never in my wildest dreams had I envisioned a young hippy fella so h-o-t, *hot*. Dear God! With long dirty-blonde hair, blue eyes, and a beard, he was a *Legends of the Falls* version of Brad Pitt. Having been a raft guide and ski instructor for most of my twenties, I'd always dated rugged, mountain-man types. Since moving to New York City a few years earlier, though, I hadn't been able to find such earthy-type guys. Until now.

After we listened to Jesus' painfully long monologue about cannibalism, ate our tiny crackers, and downed our shots of grape juice, Jesus finished the show by coming out into the crowd and touching people. He made it a point to lay his hand on all fifty of us saying, "Bless you my child" to adults and children alike. While I knew he wasn't Jesus-Jesus, only the actor playing Jesus, I couldn't help but catch the Jesus fever in the cave, now looking at him almost as a force larger than life.

When it came my turn to get touched, I was a nervous wreck. I'm sure I must have looked like someone straight out of a snake-slinging tent rival since my knees buckled the moment his strong manly hand connected with the spaghetti straps on my shoulder. Blood instantly rushed to my neck and checks, making me blush, and goose bumps popped up all over my arms. Unfortunately, our little moment together was ruined by the sound of my empty wooden shot glass hitting the floor. My poor hand just couldn't concentrate on holding it anymore. When I came back up from retrieving the shot glass, Jesus had already moved on to touching the kid beside me.

I couldn't figure out what in Jesus' name was happening to me. It's not like I was looking for God. I'd already found a new one years ago, one that didn't create a hell or send people like me to it just because we once stole a thousand dollars worth of merchandise from Disney World as a teenager. I honestly didn't care about this Jesus guy or the Bible, and yet here I was falling under his Christian spell.

Just as I was finally starting to pull myself together, Jesus came up from behind and touched me. AGAIN! Now, I don't mean to brag, but I'm the only one in that entire cave who got touched more than once. Not even the children in front of me or the two women beside me in wheelchairs got it twice. After it was all over, I went to follow him out of the cave, but I was told Jesus had to go "pray in the gardens now" (i.e. costume change in the green room). The people around me chanted "Thank you Jesus! *Thank you Jesus!*" over and over as we were escorted out another door by the pharaoh-looking guy who'd dealt out the crackers. I know this is a bit of a stretch, but at the time, part of me thought perhaps this Jesus dude had been flirting with me. He was just a man after all, and men can't help themselves sometimes.

Now that I had the Jesus fever, I was on a mission to see as much of him as possible. I went to several shows, including "The Women Who Loved Jesus." It only seemed appropriate. The stars of this show included his mom, a pissed-off hooker, some woman who was almost stoned to death by a crowd of angry men, and a lady who'd been bleeding for twelve years due to some strange, unexplained disease. You'd think after all my training I would have known my Bible stories a little better, but I was totally lost for the entire show.

If I hadn't been there to see Jesus, my feminist self would have been highly insulted by the content. One pathetic woman after another gave a long-winded speech about how no man cared about her. Then, like a superhero, Jesus would swoop in, she'd cry, he'd save the day, they'd embrace, then she'd give another speech after he left about how obsessed she was with him. They all said phrases like "I've never loved anyone the way I love *that* man," and "I think I love him in a . . . *different* way," or my personal favorite, "No man has ever touched me in *that* way."

Whenever Jesus wasn't saving some damsel in distress, he was hanging out in the streets of Jerusalem with his homies. Like John Travolta's character in *Grease*, he was the guy every man wanted to be and the hunk every woman

wanted to screw. Things took a turn for the worse, however, when out of nowhere a bunch of Roman guards ran
on stage and started flogging their hero. At the end of the
show an announcer came over the intercom and told us
not to miss the follow-up grand finale called "The Passion
of The Christ" outside in twenty minutes.

Given the sexual overtones in this last show, one might
assume "The Passion of the Christ" was going to be some
sort of soft porn, but I had a sneaky feeling it would be a
live version of that awful Mel Gibson flick. I usually have
a pretty week stomach, but I couldn't get enough of Hot
Jesus.

After all two thousand of us were herded outside and
situated behind ropes like kids awaiting a Fourth of July
parade, Jesus came out into a crowd wearing a white
robe and hippy sandals. Sweaty with a bad case of bed
head, his mood was somber as he walked around giving
another one of his long-winded speeches. Afterwards,
a group of Roman guards tackled him to the ground.
They were pretty hot themselves, each wearing gold-
plated six-pack covers and flowing skits that showed off
their soccer legs.

They dragged Jesus over to some fake rocks, where
Satan awaited him. Sporting a black robe with a hood, like
a character out of *Harry Potter*, Satan now had his chance
to make a speech. Everyone boooo-ed of course, which
pleased him greatly.

Once the guards ripped off Jesus' robe, leaving him
in an ancient Depends diaper, they bound his hands to a
wooden post with rope. If I didn't know better, I would
have thought this was some sort of old-timey S&M porno.
Each time a whip hit his back, the loudspeakers belted a
"crack" sound and fake blood magically appeared. With
every lash, Jesus violently arched his back and moaned,
sometimes even making the o-face. This amused Satan,

who laughed hysterically like he was at a taping of *Saturday Night Live.*

When they were done with the whipping part, the hot guards, now sweaty and jacked-up on testosterone, dragged Jesus out into the audience and kicked him in the kidneys repeatedly. By this point in time, my emotions were all over the place, ranging from disgust at a place that would let little kids watch such violence to fear over how un-phased the crowd was by this insanity. Then Jesus landed on all fours on the ground in front of me, covered in blood and sweat and so scantily clad I could almost see his junk through the diaper. I soon realized I was, more than anything, unbelievably horny.

But you would be too if you were a single thirty-two year old woman who hadn't had sex, much less been kissed or even touched by a man, in a year and a half. The baby-making organs of a woman in her sexual prime will latch onto anything that seems promising, even the Son of God.

It's not that I am a celibate prude. Quite the opposite in fact, I was prone to the addictive feast or famine approach to life—the one where people like me often times take a good thing too far and turn it into a bad thing. After my last binge a couple years ago, I'd decided to cage the little feline for a while. It's been pretty easy to abstain . . . until this Jesus guy showed up.

No wonder I reacted so strongly to Jesus touching me in the cave. Maybe it hadn't been a spiritual experience at all—just a sexual one. And that tent revival reaction of mine was probably just Jesus jolting awake hormones that'd been on snooze for too long. After the touching incident, the whipping, and now, here in front of me, a sweaty, handsome hippy with the body of a swimmer bent over doggy-style, my inner tiger smelled blood and desperately wanted out of her cage.

There wasn't much I could do with all this arousal other than continue to watch and take some pictures. Eventually the guards put a thorny crown on his head and made him carry a log, all the while continuing to beat him. I couldn't believe he just kept taking it, like a man, never giving up.

Once he was up on the cross, the guards pounded huge spikes through his hands and feet. (The special affects at Holy Land were some of the best I've ever seen, by the way.) They let the poor guy hang up there for quite a while, which was kind of boring to watch until one guard gave him a sponge bath and another speared Jesus in the gut. I must say, even nailed to a cross, the guy looked hot. And that six-pack! I've never been a fan of buff guys, but Jesus had one of those lean-yet-toned figures I always fell for. Sure, I felt bad staring at him "that way" while the people around me cried, but I couldn't help it. This was the first near-naked man I'd been around in ages.

I'm sure you know what happened next. He died. The guards took a hammer to his hands and feet to get the mails out, lowered his perfect body down from the cross, then wrapped him in a white sheet and carried him through the crowd down to a tomb. Satan made a victory speech, and again, the crowd booed.

After the tomb exploded, Jesus appeared again, only this time he had a wardrobe change. All cleaned-up now, he wore a white flowing nightgown, gave another speech, thanked his Dad, then held up a set of enormous golden keys in front of the crowd. Anyone who wanted keys to his place, he said, they were there for the taking. Hells yeah I wanted keys to his place! If only he wasn't speaking metaphorically.

All of a sudden, a bunch of angels dressed in white and gold disco outfits gathered around him and started twirling, like dancers at a Grateful Dead show. Their gold, sparkly wings fluttered and made cool designs, a visual routine that would have blown the mind of anyone on acid.

We were told to follow the angels to heaven, so all two thousand of us walked about fifty yards away to a gold and white amphitheater where we were met by even more dancing angels. After about ten minutes, Jesus finally showed up, casually late to his own party, only now he wore a non-thorny crown and a King's robe. As he walked down the aisles, people held their right hands up and screamed "Praise Jesus!" again and again.

Not only was the train of his robe longer than Princess Diana's wedding gown, but he had the aura of a real king. While I've never actually dated a guy with money, I'm still just as much of a sucker as any woman for a handsome man with power and loads of cash. And don't forget fame. He wasn't just the most popular man at Holy Land; he was the most famous person in the *world*. Even more so than Brad Pitt.

Satan made one more appearance, but Jesus had the upper hand now. He threw Satan on the ground by pointing his staff at him and using his superpowers. Two disco angels picked Satan up off the ground and lassoed him with a gold rope before escorting him out of Heaven, once and for all.

As the crowd continued to cheer and Jesus reveled in his glory, I started to wonder if maybe I had a shot at hooking up with him after the show. I mean, I *was* on vacation and that was usually the only time I ever hooked up with cute guys. Even though I wasn't the prettiest woman at Holy Land, the odds were definitely in my favor. There was absolutely no competition—most good, Christian women wouldn't even consider banging the Holy Spirit. And certainly not in the backseat of a car or in a public restroom like me.

After the show was over, I went looking for Hot Jesus, but he was nowhere to be found. I was willing at this point to even settle for one of the hot Roman guards, but they must have made a dash for the green room too. After wandering around, looking for *any* guy in a costume, I finally gave up on Holy Land and left. Defeated.

Back in NYC, I started noticing a dramatic change in my body. I'd be on a crowded subway or waiting in an hour-long line at Trader Joe's when, all of a sudden, I'd have that knee-buckling experience if a man so much as brushed up against me. These were not good-looking men, or men I'd even consider hooking up with. They were still men though, and I was a single, horny woman in her thirties who still hadn't been touched by anyone in almost two years, except for Jesus of course. Being a hormonal landmine of sorts, I knew I needed to do something.

One day, as if by divine intervention, a kid next to me on the subway grabbed my leg. For the entire subway ride he made sure he always had a hand on someone, if not me or his mom, then another adult close by. It occurred to me at that moment that perhaps I wasn't a horn-ball or a sex-crazed psycho, but rather a human being who just needed to be touched. The need to have physical contact with another human being doesn't go away just because we grow into adults. In fact, once I thought about it, I bet half the men I'd hooked up with in the past had been out of a dire need be hugged.

I knew then and there that I had to find another way to survive in such a dark, lonely city like New York, lest I settle for a boyfriend who's bad for me. So thanks to Jesus, I do what I think any smart single woman ought to do. I pay someone to touch me. Twice a month, I treat myself to a massage. Until, that is, I meet a guy as nice and cute as Hot Jesus.

★

Melanie Hamlett is a travel writer and two-time Moth Storyslam winner who lives in either a trailer in New Mexico, the back of her truck on the road, a friend's couch in NYC, or out of a backpack in a foreign country. She's been featured in multiple podcasts, including Risk! and Broadcastr, and can be seen performing all over New York City at places like The Upright Citizens Brigade and The Moth. She also tells picture-stories about her travels as a wandering narcoleptic at melaniehamlett.com. She's currently writing her first book about her adventures.

LORI ROBINSON

Giving Dad
the Bird

*A daughter gets her feathers ruffled and finds birds
of a feather do indeed flock together.*

SINCE I WAS A YOUNG GIRL CONVERSATIONS WITH DAD ARE
more often than not interrupted by him raising his hand
like a stop sign and announcing with great importance,
"Listen, there's a black-throated blue warbler," or some
such name. He cocks his ear toward the noise, and with
pursed lips calls out a perfect "pish, pish, pish," hoping to
entice the bird closer. A birder's universal call, this sound
can be perfected by studying *The Art of Pishing*, (audio CD
included) by Pete Dune. A copy of it, along with *What
Bird Did That?*—pictures of different windshield bird splats
accompanied by detailed descriptions of color, contents
and consistency—are among the hundred or so birding
books my dad owns. From a psychological viewpoint it's
easy to understand why I view all birds as competition for
my father's attention, and developed no interest whatso-
ever in the winged creatures.

No one is spared his avian obsession. In the middle of
a tennis match with my mother he overhears a stranger in

the adjacent court identify a bird flying overhead as a per-
egrine falcon. My dad doesn't see the bird but doubts the
accuracy of the strangers call. Off court, approaching the
other birder he asks "are you sure that wasn't a merlin?"
With a confidence that comes from birding since he was
six, he adds, "Peregrines are rarely seen here." Before the
man can answer, the same bird flies overhead again, this
time chasing an egret, proof to my dad that the stranger's
identification *is* correct. They become the best of friends,
traveling the world in search of birds.

There are two kinds of people who sign up for an African
safari. Most, myself included, want to see "The Big Five"—
lion, leopard, rhino, buffalo, and elephant. If those large
predators are engaged in a chase, or a kill, that's even better.
The other people are . . . the birders. So when my father
announces he wants to join me on a trip to South Africa
and Botswana I have planned for myself, I am delighted, but
feel I must clarify. "Dad, you know this is not a birding trip."

"Fine by me," he replies. "I won't even mention my
interest in birds to anyone so I don't interfere with any
part of your trip."

True to his word, for the first part of our journey anyway, he doesn't mention it. He doesn't need to. My dad is
never without a pair of binoculars hanging from his neck,
and a pencil and local bird list sticking out of his back
pocket, ready to identify any flying species.

At our first stop we meet up with a group of my friends
at a private reserve near Kruger National Park. An under-
current of excitement flows through my body as we
hike within yards of zebra, giraffe, baboon, and the large
antelope—kudu and red hartebeest. Some of the animals
snort, warning us we are a little too close. Others flee,
almost touching us as they gallop past. It is a special treat
to walk in the African bush without an armed guide, but

my father's thrill comes only from adding little bee-eaters and black-eyed bulbuls to his birding list.

"Where is your father?" becomes the group's mantra, and I am sure to find him, off on his own, whispering the identifying characteristics of the bird species he's filming, into the microphone of his camcorder. In the Northern Transvaal, my friends and I climb among rock cliffs where we discover fresh leopard prints in the sand. Meanwhile, Dad, wearing his favorite khaki flop hat that is one size too big, stalks lanner falcons, red-breasted hornbills, and gray lourie's. The group cooks stew and bread in a three-legged "Potjie Pot" over an open fire, while under the stars our guide talks about the history of the area, and dad checks off boxes on his birding list. He is especially excited by "lifers"; those birds he has never seen before. Near the Limpopo River, I crawl into caves to look at paintings of elongated giraffe like animals, and funny faced distorted bodies drawn hundreds of years ago by the earliest bushman. My father videos brown snake eagles, red-winged starlings, and violet-eared waxbills.

For the most anticipated part of my itinerary, Dad and I fly alone to Botswana to visit two different lodges chosen because of their large populations of my favorite animals—cats and elephants. Wrapped in blankets against the 5:30 A.M. chill, we climb into the open Land Rover for our first wildlife drive. Impatient to get into the bush (I haven't been to Africa for ten years), I hardly hear Tim, our driver guide, recite the do's and don'ts of safari etiquette. *I wish he would stop talking so we could get going as not to miss any early morning big game sightings.*

Finally, Tim finishes his spiel. "So let's push off," he says.

"Yes," I concur, with an enthusiastic clap of my hands.

But before he starts the engine, he turns again toward my father and me in the back seat and asks, "Are either of you birders?"

Why do they always ask that?

"I'm not," I respond with an *I'm in charge* attitude, hoping Tim realizes I am speaking for my father and myself. "I want to focus on mammals, especially lions and elephants."

Then my father murmurs something about . . . "birder," followed by: "But this is my daughter's trip and I don't want to ruin it for her, so lets focus on large animals."

As I'm thinking *how sweet it is of him to say that*, I hear him add, "But if we see a bird or two that would be great." *A bird or two? Is he joking? Birds are everywhere, they're inescapable.*

Tim's face lights up as if he just caught up with a long lost friend, "Oh wonderful, I'm a birder too," he says. From the detail with which Tim and his new best buddy then compare binoculars, I realize I'm doomed.

It's known amongst safari tour operators in Africa that drivers are happiest when they have birding clients. I'm not sure why. Maybe it's because although birds are everywhere, they are difficult to get a good look at, so the drivers have to work harder, and they get tipped accordingly. Or, after years of pointing out mammals, complacent drivers find a rewarding challenge in pointing out a rarely or never seen bird from the hundreds of species on this continent. But I really don't know the exact reasons that drivers love clients who are birders because I always avoid those vehicles in favor of the groups looking for "real" wildlife.

A few minutes into our drive we stop. I scan the area, but see nothing. Tim is pointing and to the left of us I catch a glimpse of purple, green, yellow, orange, and blue feathers shimmering in the first morning light. *This is a beautiful bird,* I admit to myself. *O.K., I've seen it, let's move on.* The lilac-breasted roller is a lifer for my father, and he wants to see the male roll earthward from the sky in his mating dance. *Oh great, now we have a specific goal for the day's outing.*

During our two-hour drive we stop more than a school bus full of kids. We halt and stare at every brown, blue, yellow, big, little, flying and sitting bird. I listen to discussions of wing-spans, beak shapes and throat colors, and I learn new names like Hammerkop and Bateleur.

An hour and a half, and twelve lilac-breasted roller sightings later, we see a pride of seven lion, sleeping belly up, their baseball mitt-size paws facing the sky. *Finally!* I rest my elbows on the edge of the vehicle's door for a more comfortable viewing position, and focus my father's hand-me-down binoculars on their blood stained, fly covered fur. The lions' twitching whiskers, and the way their full bellies move up and down with each breath, are riveting.

After a few minutes, Tim interrupts my big cat trance, "They aren't going to do anything, so let's push onward."

So we can find some more birds which are doing so much, I think to myself. *I would rather spend the rest of the day watching these lions sleep.*

Our remaining four wildlife drives at Chitabe Camp follow the same pattern. My needs to see things larger than an eagle are accommodated, but lack the obvious enthusiasm that accompanies any and all bird sightings. I have practically become a birder myself by osmosis alone, so at our next lodge, with only two days left before we go home, I am not taking any chances. I explain to my father, "It is probably obvious by the name of the lodge, Savute Elephant Camp that I really want to focus on elephants here."

"Yes, of course," he agrees. *I've heard that before.* For added assurance I find a private guide to lead us on a big-game walking experience.

"We have no interest in seeing birds," I tell Clive when I hire him. He mentions a rogue bull elephant in the area. "We will try to find him," he says.

"Perfect," I agree. *This man has my interests in mind.*

In single file I follow Clive and the shotgun slung over his right shoulder; my father behind me. When we catch up to the massive gray young bull, Clive hand motions us to go slow, be quiet, and stay close to him.

He whispers, "Adolescent male elephants are ousted from the matriarchal herd to find a new group where they can mate, so they can be unpredictable and dangerous."

Clive signals us to stop; any farther and we would be too close for comfort. The bull moves from one mopane tree to the next, snapping branches like twigs and stripping the red leaves, seemingly oblivious to his audience of three. As I turn to share this adrenaline pumping moment with my dad, the massive creature begins to walk away. At the same moment, Clive and I realize Dad is nowhere in sight.

"We can't follow the elephant until we find your father; I don't want him getting lost out here," Clive insists. I know he is right, but I'm reluctant to let the elephant get any farther away from us.

Turning around I can see my father in the distance, half hidden behind a thick bush, video camera leading him in the opposite direction from the elephant and us. His lens is focused on a tree branch, on top of which sits a lilac-breasted roller.

Catching up to him, I plead, "Dad, you have seen hundreds of lilac-breasted rollers already, please can you walk with us, the elephant's getting away."

"You've seen a hundred elephants already," he retaliates. We stare at each other for a tension filled moment, and then we both start to laugh. The noise startles the bird and it flies off, while my elephant disappears into thick bush.

Back home in the States my father sends me a gift for including him on my African journey. I unwrap the package to find a two-by-three-foot poster of a lilac-breasted roller.

He will make a birder out of me yet.

★

When she isn't traveling and leading safaris in Africa, Lori Robinson lives in Santa Barbara, California. She writes and blogs about her thirty years of traveling to eleven (so far) African countries. Find her online at www.AfricaInside.org.

KIRSTEN KOZA

Easter Island and the Chilean with the Brazilian

Travel is so broadening and
occasionally eye-popping.

My obsession with Easter Island's mysterious monolithic stone statues started when I was around five-years-old after I'd seen the film *Chariots of the Gods*. In the movie, aliens had helped the natives of Easter Island erect stone monoliths called Moai. Of course I now know that aliens had nothing to do with the Moai—I mean, come on, if extraterrestrials could build a space ship to fly across galaxies, surely they'd do something else with their spare time besides helping scantily clad Polynesians carve rudimentary cement-truck-sized statues on one of the most remote inhabited islands in the world, 3000 miles off the coast of Chile.

Finally, forty years later, I was hiking up Rano Raraku volcano, the birth place of the Moai, with my seven-year-old son, Rigel. I pulled my collar up to protect my neck from the ruthless sun and pulled my hat down over my face to hide my already blistered lips. No shade in sight, the Rapa Nui natives had eviscerated the island of trees to transport their statues across the volcanic terrain. I recognized individual Moai from Thor Heyerdahl's book. I was about as close to Nirvana as I could get. Rigel and I continued up slowly.

"Can we go to the beach now? It's hot," Rigel gasped.

I looked at his little scarlet face and then the giant Moai lying stacked upon one another, still in the midst of being carved out of the volcano's walls but frozen in process by an outbreak of tribal war, which was followed by despair and cannibalism, and then an invasion of slave traders in the 1800s. "Yeah, O.K.," I agreed. We had three weeks here, so no rush. I'd hang with Rigel. I looked around for my husband, Malcolm, and my friend Karen who'd gone ahead.

Rigel and I descended the dust-slick rock path. We ended up stuck behind two Chilean women in high-heeled beach sandals (stiletto flip flops). Their skirts were flapping in the strong breeze and their tight-jeaned man, equally encumbered by his attire was failing dismally at helping either lady down the slope.

"Excuse me, excuse us," I said as Rigel and I skidded past the traffic jam of frills and girly-girls clutching their cologne soaked he-man.

As I helped Rigel climb down a steep rock below one of the Chilean princesses, her dress blew up like Marilyn Monroe's—except this wasn't family rated. I saw Rigel's face blanch and his pupils dilate.

Rigel leapt towards me, grabbed my hand, and pulled me down the steep incline at break-neck speed. "Why did that woman's vagina look like that?"

Oh, God.

"Her vagina hair was just a thin black stripe," Rigel said in shock.

I hoped this was not going to be his first journal entry in his Easter Island Diary that he was bringing back to his grade one teacher and class. As it was, the teacher disapproved of me taking Rigel out of school for a three week trip. She thought his life might be adversely affected by missing that much cut and paste and carpet time.

"Did her hair on her vagina grow into that shape?"

"No, she's had it waxed." *Shit.*

"Like a car?" Rigel asked. "Is that why her vagina was so shiny?"

"No, that was tanning oil or something."

"Why would she want a wax and tan on her vagina?"

"Rigel, you see that Moai over there. His name is El Gigante and he weighs over four hundred thousand pounds." I pointed to the resting giant. "He was someone's real great great-great granddad, as all the Moai were shaped and carved for real Rapa Nui people."

"Where is she from?" Rigel inquired.

"Huh?" I looked at El Gigante. It would have taken an entire tribe or clan a whole year to carve this.

Rigel tugged my arm. "What country is that woman from?"

"She's Chilean," I said.

"Do people from different countries have pubic hair that grows in different shapes?"

Oh, great. "No, she's had most of her pubic hair removed." I stopped myself from going any further. We were at one of the world's greatest archaeological wonders and I wasn't about to give my son a lesson on bikini waxing styles.

"Can you pick the shape you want your pubic hair to be? Do you ever do that to yours?"

"No!"

"Hers was a zebra."

"It was a Brazilian," I said.

"Why would a Chilean want a Brazilian on her vagina?" Rigel asked.

Later, my friend Karen and I stood in the soft white sand below the Moai, at Anakena beach, while my husband took over cooking lunch in a large Rapa Nui woman's beach kiosk. Anakena was where the Rapa Nui canoes had first arrived, after their treacherous 2,400 mile paddle across the South Pacific, from the Marquesas Islands. Rigel ran around impatiently as we took pictures.

"I can't believe we're here," said Karen. "It's incredible. I never fathomed the size of the monoliths or how hard it must have been to transport them around the island."

"Karen," I whispered. "It's a good thing you educated me all the varieties of pubic epilation the other day. It came in handy at Rano Raraku."

"Why?" Karen asked, moving her sunglasses down her nose to look at me.

"A couple of Chilean women were going commando and Rigel had frontal view of beaver."

Karen laughed. "So which style was it?"

"It was a Brazilian beaver."

"Full? As in the naked Sphinx?" Karen inquired.

"No, there was a landing strip."

Karen laughed even louder. "Hey Rigel," Karen called. "Did you know that one of the statues' hats weighs as much as two elephants?"

Rigel ran over. He was excited. "Mom, Karen, guess what?"

"What?"

"That Chilean woman is here!"

★

Kirsten Koza is the author of the memoir, Lost in Moscow. *She is a Canadian travel writer, playwright, speaker and humorist.*

KATHLEEN K. MILLER

Why You Worry?

This was not the Jungle Cruise she had in mind.

EVERY NOW AND THEN, MY MOTHER WILL ASK ME WHAT I actually *did* in the two years that I spent in South America. The scene that immediately pops into my mind is an image of me sitting in a canoe in the middle of the night in the Amazon jungle, surrounded by strange men, while our tour guide (wearing only an orange Speedo and completely inebriated) waved around a deadly poisonous snake that he had tied to a stick. So I smile and tell her that I spent a lot of time in nature reserves.

I thought I loved nature. I love hiking, I love being outdoors, I love animals (especially of the cuddly variety, like puppies and baby goats—you know, petting zoo animals). I think mountains are spectacular and I love the ocean. I thought a tour in the Amazon would be beautiful. Get back to nature, spend some time outdoors, escape from the stress of modern-day living for a while, and maybe try to break my addiction to Facebook for a few days. So when the smooth-talking travel agent told me that the best way to really experience the jungle was on a five-day tour, I said, "That sounds excellent!" A little pricey, perhaps, but surely it was worth it to *really* experience the Amazon? The stuff of

National Geographic and BBC specials, up close and personal. What an experience! Bragging rights for a lifetime!

I forgot one crucial, crucial detail: the Amazon is no petting zoo. The closest thing to a "cuddly" animal is a wild sloth with surprisingly sharp claws. The Amazon, while it does boast beautiful birds and river scenery, is also the home of the bird-eating tarantula, glow-in-the-dark beetles, deadly spiders, ants whose bites will leave you temporarily paralyzed while they eat your eyeballs, and hordes of dengue-and-malaria-ridden mosquitoes. The climate is not particularly pleasant either, unless you're a fan of one hundred percent humidity and have a penchant for pit stains.

I was picked up from my hostel and met a few of the other tourists who would be joining me: a Brazilian who was only on a day trip (what a weakling), an Argentinian couple who were doing an overnight trip (hmmm) and two Swedish guys who were doing a four-day trip (wait a minute). That was the first "oh, shit" moment: when I realized that I was the only person signed up for five days. Why was it that everyone else, including the hard-core backpackers like myself, was willing to skip out early?

This became a little clearer when we arrived at the floating lodge. It was modest: a green building, indeed floating, anchored in place with ropes tied to the huge trees that lined the river. No electricity, simple accommodations, excellent for my spiritual return to nature. Our guide, Joshua, sat down with us at a wooden table that immediately reminded me of Girl Scout Day Camp, from when I was about the age of seven, and started going over how long everyone would be staying. One day, two days, four days . . . "And who signed up for the jungle survivor trip?" He asked. No one answered. He checked his list again. "It says it's an American . . . ." All eyes went to me.

"Excuse me?" I said.

"I have you down here for the survivor trip. Five days, right?"

I searched my memory. What had the guy from the travel agency called my trip? Had he used the word "survivor" in his description? He couldn't have, there was no way I would have been stupid enough to sign up for a "survivor tour"... or did I? I couldn't remember the exact words, it had been so hot in that office and I had been so thirsty. I mustered some kind of incomprehensible squeak, which Joshua interpreted as an affirmative response. "O.K. then! Let's go piranha fishing."

The afternoon was pleasant: piranha fishing was interesting enough, although I was reprimanded by Joshua several times for not concentrating and failing to pay enough attention to my fishing line, as the piranhas stole all my bait and evaded my hook. I eventually managed to catch two, at which point I immediately began to feel bad for the piranhas and remembered that I hated fishing. Minus one point for my return to nature.

We returned to the lodge for a fish dinner with spaghetti (funny how fish and spaghetti seemed to be considered complementary menu items in Brazil), and then went on a nighttime tour of the river. The scenery was, indeed, beautiful. The water in the smaller tributaries was still, and in the dark, it looked like a black mirror reflecting the stars and shoreline. We were surrounded by silence, except for the stir of the wind on the leaves and the hiss of insects.

I, however, was preoccupied for the duration of the nighttime tour: I was trying to scheme up a good excuse to leave after Day 4, when the Swedish tourists were also leaving. Bum foot? (I did have an impressive-looking ankle brace and ace bandage with me from an injury, and an authentic limp.) Family emergency? No good, how would I have found out about a family emergency in the middle of the Amazon without internet or electricity? Fear of the jungle? No, I had more pride than that. Vague and embarrassing woman disease? Not to be ruled out.

I was only distracted from my brainstorming when Joshua docked the boat in a dark, swampy area surrounded by trees almost entirely submerged in water. Since it was the rainy season, the water was high: it was like being in a flood zone, with fully-formed tree trunks and branches at eye level. Joshua jumped out of the boat. "O.K.," he said with thickly accented English, "I go catch alligator. Wait here."

As the five of us exchanged looks ("Wait, did he just say he's going to bring back an alligator?"), he shouted back, "And no talking!"

O.K. No talking. We waited in the boat, all of us painfully aware of the extremely hard wooden benches uncomfortably digging into our asses. I dozed off for a bit. It was a little eerie, this swamp. Pitch black dark, except for Joshua's flashlight bobbing in the distance as he swam and waded through the trees. Vines hanging down, one of which I was carefully leaning away from because there was a spider hanging on it. After an eternity of forty minutes, Joshua returned: in one hand, he held a forked stick with a snake tied to it; in the other, a baby alligator. Holy shit.

"O.K., O.K.! This snake kill many people every year. So no touch head of snake. You want to hold?"

Fuck no, I don't want to hold! And if it kills many people every year, why the fuck are you waving it around the inside of this boat? I heard Joachim, one of the Swedes, murmur from the back of the boat, "Was this included in the waiver?" Waiver, I thought frantically, did I sign a waiver? Or, more importantly, did they ask me about any health concerns or problems I might have? Does this boat even have a first-aid kit?

"Joshua," I said, throwing tact to the wind, "are the guides here trained in first aid?"

"Why you worry? Everything fine. Someone get bit, I give them jungle medicine."

Oh, excellent. If I get bit by a deadly poisonous snake, a man wearing a bright orange Speedo swimsuit will give me jungle medicine.

Now, as a newbie to the jungle, I learned a very important lesson that night. The best way to survive in the jungle is through a careful combination of alcohol and pharmaceuticals. I was only foolish enough to spend one sober night in the jungle: the first one. I spent the night tossing and turning in my room, sweating from the heat and waking up every half hour to spray more DEET on my skin and wishing I had gone for the 100 percent. At this point, I didn't care if I had mutant children because of the carcinogens in my insect repellent: I just wanted these monster-mosquitoes to leave me alone. After that first restless night, I embraced the philosophies of all our guides, who (while they claimed to love nature and their jobs) drank their weight in alcohol on a nightly basis. And it made sense: who wants to remember that they're surrounded by all that nature *all the time*? Certainly not me. I definitely, absolutely and unequivocally preferred to be intoxicated as soon as the sun went down. Yes, the tarantulas, and scary nights, and bugs, and anacondas were still *there*, but I didn't give a shit if I had a few shots of cachaça. And this was how Joachim and Nicklas, the two Swedes, became my friends. We passed the second night drinking at the lodge, downing glass after glass of cachaça and Fanta. Interestingly enough, the cachaça cost a third as much as the soda we mixed it with. It says something about an establishment when their alcohol is cheaper than their water.

The following day, though it began with a rather brutal hangover (more difficult to overcome than usual—it's hard to stay hydrated in that kind of heat), was off to a solid start. At least we had all gotten some sleep. Nicklas, Joachim, and myself were the only tourists left in our group, and we were treated to a canoe ride through some of the backwaters in the hopes of seeing some of the more elusive animals.

"There," Joshua said. "Up there. You see sloth?"

The three of us stared at the incomprehensible tangle of branches and leaves.

"No," I said bluntly.

"O.K. O.K. You wait here."

Joshua tied the boat to the tree, and before any of us could say anything, he had jumped out of the canoe and began scaling the tree. He had an extremely uncanny ability to climb trees: he seemed more monkey than human in that respect.

"Jesus," I said, as he disappeared from sight, "he's like some kind of superhuman."

"What's he doing?" Joachim asked, craning his head. "He's not catching the sloth, is he?"

"No way," I said. "He wouldn't."

"I bet he would," Niklas countered.

As we debated the matter, we heard Joshua talking—presumably to the sloth—in the trees above our heads. "Come here, baby, come here," I heard him murmur in Portuguese. The next thing we knew, we saw Joshua lowering the sloth—which he had tied to some kind of cloth harness—down towards the canoe, as Joshua climbed back down the tree.

"Oh my god," I said. "He didn't."

But he had. The sloth was actually kind of cute, if you could look past its enormous claws. Or get over the fact that our guide had just captured an innocent animal that, according to Joshua, was "very, very angry." To me, the sloth looked completely expressionless; kind of like a teddy bear. It made some kind of brief, low noise. "Sloth very angry," Joshua said cheerfully, poking it in the head, "very angry."

"Of course it's angry," Niklas whispered. "We're . . . we're *violating* it!"

The three of us were torn between guilt and an incredible photo opportunity. We settled for photos of us guiltily holding the sloth, all three of us taking turns holding it up by the harness, each with a pained expression on our face.

"The title of this Facebook album is going to be 'the violation of the sloth,'" I whispered to Nicklas and Joachim.

"Poor thing's never going to get over it," Joachim said. "Do you think sloths can have post-traumatic stress disorder?"

"How would you tell?" Nicklas asked. "Would it move an entire inch, instead of the fraction of the inch it moved when it was really pissed just now?"

"It's going to take it *weeks* to get back up in that tree, at the rate it's going now," Joachim said. We all stared at the sloth, completely immobile; it hadn't even moved its paw from where Joshua had left it on the tree.

"O.K. O.K.!" Joshua said, completely unperturbed by remorse, "I go catch baby monkey now."

"No!" the three of us shouted, almost simultaneously. "Joshua, no baby monkey," I protested. "That's just too close to human for me."

Joshua shrugged. "O.K. O.K. We go to bar now."

The "bar," it turned out, was a shack on the river that sold alcohol. Joshua drank what had to be the equivalent of six or seven shots of vodka, straight up. The man had a tolerance. Meanwhile, the bartender tried to speak to me, but I had trouble understanding his Portuguese. Joshua interceded, his voice slightly slurred.

"He's trying to tell you," Joshua told me in Spanish, "that there was another blonde girl here a few weeks ago. She died, though."

"Oh," I said, trying to decide if I wanted any further details. I decided that I didn't.

"What's he saying?" Niklas asked me.

"Don't worry about it," I said hastily.

The bartender went on to explain, via Joshua's translation, that most tourists don't visit this particular bar. "Too hard to find," he said. "Most tour guides get lost in the tributaries around here and can't find their way back."

"Joshua," I said, "do you know how to get back?"

"Why you worry? This girl always worry," he told the bartender, taking another swig of vodka.

I continued to worry, twenty minutes later, as a little bit of rain turned into a torrential downpour. I could barely see a few feet in front of my face because of the rain. I huddled on the floor of the canoe, terrified of the lightning that seemed to be directly over our heads. I had very little faith in Joshua's abilities to find his way back to the lodge when he was completely drunk, with poor visibility and a quickly darkening sky on top of it.

"Are you O.K.?" Joachim asked from a few feet above me, as I quaked on the floor of the canoe.

"I'm fantastic," I muttered, my voice muffled by the fact that I was hiding my face in my hands, silently uttering Hail Marys and wishing I had left more details about my whereabouts with my family. "Tell me when it's over."

Much to my disbelief, Joshua did manage to find his way back to the lodge, and the Swedes and I retreated to another night of cachaça and Fanta.

"O.K.," Joshua said the next morning. "Today we go camping in jungle. This group small, so new people will join tour." He gestured toward the four Russians who had arrived at the lodge the day before. The Russians, it seemed, had an aversion to both sobriety and clothing. I had yet to see any of them sober (in fact, right now they were pouring vodka into their orange juice with breakfast), and as far as I could tell, the only clothing they had brought with them were Speedo swimsuits.

They did seem to be having an inordinate amount of fun on their Amazon tour, though. They continued drinking and smoking pot throughout the day, as we visited a banana plantation and took off on a boat for our campsite. Our departure was delayed slightly when one of the Russians, completely inebriated, accidentally jumped from the dock and landed in the river instead of in the boat. Joshua and the other tour guide who had joined our group fished him out without incident, while the other three laughed and poured him more vodka.

To their credit, the Russians were incredibly pleasant to be around. Loud, drunk, and barely clothed, they were endlessly entertaining. The Swedes and I declined their offers of alcohol and pot ("Katy," one of them told me, in a thick accent, "If you like, you can smoke") and amused ourselves by watching them. The Swedes and I were covered from head to foot in long-sleeved shirts and long pants as protection against the mosquitoes and venomous insects. The Russians had no such concerns; while the Swedes and I sat gingerly on tree trunks, carefully searching them for poisonous spiders first, all four Russians passed out on the ground, wearing nothing but their Speedos. At one point, one of them disappeared into the jungle for a bathroom break; after twenty minutes, we realized that he had truly disappeared. Our guides had to do a full-on search before they returned with him another twenty minutes later, warning him against wandering off and falling asleep when in a dangerous jungle.

Maybe it was passing such a pleasant evening with the Swedes, watching the Russians stumble around the jungle, that gave me a false sense of confidence and made me believe that I was enjoying myself. I was enjoying good company, true. I was *not* enjoying the monstrously sized mosquitoes, or sleeping in a hammock with no protection from whatever roamed the jungle at night, or the fear that I would be strangled by an anaconda every time I slipped off into the wilderness to pee. I was also vaguely aware that staying that last day after the Swedes' departure might appear to be a bad idea to some people (namely, my parents, close friends, and anyone who with a scrap of common sense). I would, after all, be the only woman in the lodge. On the other hand, my pride prevented me from leaving early, and I had already paid for my last day at the lodge. Besides, I had reluctantly decided that it was pretty peaceful hanging out on the river.

And that was how I ended up on Day 5 of the Survivor Tour. The last day, it turned out, wasn't anything particularly exciting or dangerous: my guides gave me the options of going alligator or wild boar hunting, but I declined in favor of going on another canoe ride with the new tour group. My new group consisted of John, an American graduate student, and a German-American man named Magnus who had lived in San Diego for fifty years but had the strongest German accent I've ever heard. This canoe ride was much less uneventful; our guide was a man named Michael who wore a camouflage T-shirt emblazoned with the words "Soldier For Jesus" on it. Michael didn't seem inclined to catch any sloths or baby monkeys, much to my relief. We did, however, visit a beautiful jungle lodge about an hour down the river.

"If you ever come back to the Amazon," Michael said, "You should stay here."

Then we paused for a few minutes to appreciate the beauty of the competition. I took an extra moment to appreciate the irony of a jungle tour company that flat-out acknowledges their complete lack of repeat business, and goes as far as to make recommendations for future trips.

That night, we went to a different location for the campsite. "Katy's already seen the other campsite," Michael explained. As if there was something to see at the campsites—once our guides had cleared an area in the dense forest, it was like being surrounded by walls of foliage. Again, not very eco-friendly, what with the deforestation and all, but perhaps this was why they didn't anticipate any repeat visits.

I have to admit, though, that I was feeling pretty bad-ass, being the only person in the tour who had ever camped in the Amazon before. Sure, there were only three of us, and sure, it had only been once the night before, but I was the veteran of the group, and I savored my authority. Or I did until our boat landed, and I was expected to help build our shelter for the evening. I thought wistfully of the Swedes, who had done all the work the previous day (the Russians had swung around on the branches like monkeys, and although they seemed to interpret this as helpful, the Swedes still did all the work). We built a rough frame to hang the hammocks on, which seemed to be a rather precarious sleeping arrangement, but Michael assured me that it would be fine.

"We can swim by the waterfall," he suggested as I wiped the sweat off my brow.

"I don't have a swimsuit."

"We just go with no clothes, then."

"When hell freezes over."

Magnus, meanwhile, was not very happy about the camping arrangements.

"Vhat the hell is this?" he said in disgust, his German accent sounding angrier than usual as he stared at the hammock arrangements. "I did not pay to sleep like crap in this . . . *hovel.*"

When Michael began protesting, Magnus held up his hand and shook his head. "Don't vorry, don't vorry. I vill just take some Valium."

Michael turned out to be a much more considerate tour guide than Joshua; for starters, he carved us all wooden spoons to eat our dinner with. "Let me see yours?" John said.

"Hey Michael," John said, "how come my spoon isn't carved with 'Marry me my love?'"

"Shut up," I muttered, snatching my spoon back and glaring at Michael. Michael, undeterred, pulled out his guitar (or some kind of similar instrument) and began singing love songs.

"I think you're being serenaded," John whispered, standing up. As he stood, he smacked the back of his head against one of the logs jutting out from the hammock structure. "Vatch it!" Magnus shouted. "I am trying to *rest*. Vhat is so hard to understand about that?"

Michael ignored him and began singing a creation story, which talked about the world beginning in the jungle and people spreading across the world from the Amazon. It was a beautiful song, and I closed my eyes to listen to it.

I was broken out of my reverie within moments by Magnus. "I'm sorry, my friend," Magnus shouted from the hammock, "But that's crap. The world didn't begin in the Amazon. There is scientific evidence to the contrary. The human race was born in Africa."

Michael's playing faltered briefly. "It is my story," he said determinedly. "It is our creation."

"Nope, it's crap," Magnus said. "Bull crap. Not true. Fictional. Ask anyvone. Load of uneducated bull crap."

"Hey, Magnus," I said. "Shut up."

"Maybe he'll pass out from mixing Valium with cachaça," John whispered hopefully.

"Michael, it's a beautiful song," I said firmly. "Keep playing."

Michael's eyes lit up with the praise and switched to a song about undying love. "Haha," John laughed, "looks like you're a sucker."

The night continued with guitar playing and the three men drinking cachaça. I politely declined, thinking that the last thing I needed was alcohol provided by my enamored tour guide.

That was before I met The Spider. I excused myself to brush my teeth and take my malarial pills, and when I reached into my backpack, I felt my hand brush against something fuzzy. When I shined my headlight on my pack, what I saw made me scream bloody murder. It was a bird-eating tarantula. Its body was the size of my fist, the whole spider the size of my face. It was monstrous. It was furry. And it was *in my backpack*.

When I screamed, Michael, Magnus, and John came running. I stuttered incoherently, almost in tears. "Spider," I said, "spider spider spider spider *spider*."

The three of them looked around. "I don't see anything," John said. The spider, of course, had crept away as soon as I emitted my blood-curdling scream.

"Spider," I said weakly.

"I thought snake *kill* you," Michael said. "I thought you were bit."

"No. Worse," I gasped breathlessly, my hands against my heart (which seemed to be thumping in my throat), and my entire body shaking from head to toe. "Spider."

"Want some cachaça?" John asked, handing me the bottle.

Throwing sobriety to the wind, I swallowed four chugs of cachaça.

"Yes, that'll calm you down," Magnus said approvingly. "Very good, very good, have one more."

I'm not making any claims that the following events were unrelated to the cachaça consumption. I'll admit that there was probably a direct correlation. In my defense, all I have to say is that it was a very large spider, and I dare anyone to have a spider of that size brush against their hand, and see how they feel about sleeping next to it. I firmly maintain that *anyone* would consume some kind of mind-altering substance if they found themselves in that situation.

We sat next to the campfire, talking and joking, for the next hour or so. Magnus was right; the cachaça did calm me down. When it was finally time to go to bed, all four of us stood up. Michael, Magnus, and John managed to do so without incident. When I stood up, though, I did so quickly, and smacked the back of my skull—hard—on the same log that John had hit his head on earlier.

The next thing I knew, I was lying on the floor of the jungle—the same floor that the spider undoubtedly occupied—and staring up into the faces of the three men. *"Spider,"* my brain told my body, *"Spider spider spider. Spiders live here, you need to get up!"*

My body, however, was unwilling to cooperate. "Owww," I groaned. "Fuck." Michael and John both exchanged a look, clearly wondering if they were allowed to touch me, since I was the only woman and clearly drunk.

"Help me up," I snapped, sitting up dizzily.

It was hard to tell which of my problems were results of a near-concussion, and which resulted from the cachaça, since dizziness, nausea, and headache could all be attributed to either. (Especially since this particular cachaça was barely a step above rubbing alcohol.) I had a lump the size of a golf ball on the back of my head, though, and that seemed to be directly related to the injury. I stayed awake for another hour, vaguely remembering that you weren't supposed to sleep with a concussion. I stared at the fire, furious with myself for getting into this stupid situation and being on this stupid Amazon tour with these stupid spiders and stupid people and this stupid jungle. When I was fairly certain that I was in no danger of sleeping my way into a coma, I made my way towards my hammock.

As I eased my aching body into my hammock, I heard a loud crack. The way we had constructed our hammock structure meant that all four hammocks were hanging from the same log. This meant that when I got into the hammock, the structure now had to support the weight of all four of us. But it was my weight—*my weight*—that caused the entire structure to collapse.

I desperately grabbed at the hammock next to me as I plummeted towards the ground. Unfortunately, this meant that I pulled myself towards Magnus, and fell almost directly on top of him as the frame went down.

There was a brief moment of silence as the four of us lay there on the ground. Then, as I struggled to untangle myself from my hammock and Magnus, I heard a voice with a German accent.

"Normally," Magnus said furiously, his voice slightly slurred from Valium and sleeping pills, "I vould *love* to have a girl like you falling into bed vith me. *This* is the exception!"

It was not a group of happy campers that had to wake up in the middle of the night to rebuild the hammock structure.

We ate breakfast in hung over silence, and made our way back to the lodge. As I boarded the boat to return to Manaus, thinking about my jungle tour and my back-to-nature experience, all I could think was, "Never again." Until, that is, the next time that I found myself in a remote wilderness; should I find myself in Africa or Asia, I admitted to John, I would probably do another wilderness tour. Even a survivor tour.

★

Kathleen K. Miller is currently a medical student at the University of Iowa. Much to her mother's alarm and chagrin, she spent two years traveling and living in Latin America, and has also spent time in East Africa and Europe. In the future, she hopes to find time to continue traveling and writing, and eventually work in global health.

Thunda Chicken Blong Jesus Christ

Speak clearly and carry a big shtick.

"Are you sure this is a road?"

"No," Mike answered, continuing to navigate the decrepit pickup along what might have been a road.

In the periphery of incandescent green I spied movement, something between a hop and full flight.

"What was that?" I asked.

"I think it was a chicken."

"A wild, jungle chicken?"

"I guess so."

The jungle gave way and gardens flanked us. We entered a village where children, dogs, chickens and pigs milled about as we parked the truck.

"Hello," Mike spoke to a man who emerged, machete in hand, from one of the dwellings. "Is the Chief here?"

With his machete the man gestured to a makeshift house along a path. We thanked him with excessive smiles. Facing a stranger who wields a two-foot knife compels one to convey good will.

Machetes in Vanuatu are like mobile phones in the rest of the world. Everyone has one, kids included. They are for sale in hardware stores, grocery stores and at gas stations, and come in a variety of sizes (My First Machete, His-and-Her Machetes, The Granddaddy of All Machetes, etc). In a place where the foliage grows supernaturally fast and dense, it's handy to have a large knife with which to hack your way home from the office.

We made our way down the path, but the Chief emerged from his home before we reached his door, our presence having been heralded by curious children. The Chief was a squat man, no more than five foot, with a sizeable afro. He wore flip-flops, frayed denim cut-offs and an unbuttoned shirt with a bright orange floral print from which his large belly protruded.

"Hello, Mista Mike!" he exclaimed, approaching us rapidly and with open arms.

"Hello, Chief." Mike extended his arm for a handshake, which the Chief used to pull him into a bear hug. "This is my wife Amanda," Mike gasped as the air was pressed from his lungs.

"Hello, Amanda!" As the Chief enveloped me I noticed a tiny green spider crawling in his hair. I debated plucking it out for him or letting him know, but decided to let it go. Such creatures were a part of life.

"It is so nice to see you!" the Chief exclaimed, then giggled with the bashful *tee-hee* of a little girl.

"I was wondering if we might talk to some of your people about renting their canoes," Mike explained.

"Of course!" cried the Chief, "Let us go to the tree!" The Chief never spoke without a joyous exclamation point and he periodically clapped out of sheer delight.

A band of small children joined us and swung from Mike as if he were a living jungle gym. We made our way to a large metal pipe, about three feet in length and two feet in diameter, resting against the tree. The Chief picked up a smaller piece of metal and banged on the pipe, also known as the town bell. While the ni-Van, as the locals are called, emerged and studied us, the tropical heat brought my sweat-mustache into a continuous and full bloom. I dabbed at it self-consciously and began taking pictures of the town's canoes, trees that had been hollowed out enough to float a family from one island to the next.

The predominant language was Bislama, a pidgin with obvious French and English influences. Often decipherable, the Chief stepped in to translate when needed. After taking stock of the available watercraft, we left amid a cacophony of "tankyu tu mas," Bislama for "thank you very much." It's hard not to smile when someone hits you with "tankyu tu mas."

"No," I'd respond emphatically, "tank*yu* tu mas!"

Film work brought us to this archipelago of live volcanoes in the South Pacific, not far from Fiji. At the airport, my first indication of native life was a group of tambourine-wielding women, clad in dresses of a matching floral print, cheerfully singing their greeting to arriving passengers.

"You don't get a welcome like that every day," I said to Mike.

A shuttle took us to our hotel, where we were again greeted by a chorus, this time a group of tambourine-wielding men, clad in shirts of a matching floral print. This would be our welcome . . . every day. The man at the reception counter handed us each a cocktail and Vanuatu secured a special place in my heart.

We spent three months working in various coves on the island of Efaté, the one that Cook called Sandwich, scouting for canoes, deckhands and hardware needed by the film crew. During our stint, the ni-Van trained for an annual relay race circling the island. Half of the competitors I witnessed ran barefoot. Others donned flip-flops and a select few sported sneakers. The surface underneath them changed from hard-packed dirt to pavement to loose gravel, and the runners, of both sexes and varying ages, never seemed to notice. I can't walk to my mailbox barefoot; I am unable to fathom running around an island.

While the ni-Van toughened their soles for the relay, Mike's mobility slowed markedly. I thought he was embracing the relaxed pace of island life, but he grew lopsided as days passed.

"Mike, why are you limping?" I asked.

"Oh, I just have a little cut on my foot," he answered.

"Let me see it."

"No."

"Why not?"

"Because I don't want to show you."

"Is it that bad?"

"No."

"Then show me."

"No."

"Stop saying that!" I yelled. "We are married and you have to show me!"

After two weeks of insisting that marriage vows included a clause of full wound disclosure, he relented. The skin on the pad of his foot and the underside of his toes was simply missing. The raw flesh that remained, along with the fact that he had been walking on it for so long, made me shudder.

"Holy crap, I did not need to see *that*," I said.

"Well I told you," he said.

The flesh-eating infection detracted somewhat from the island's mystique. Vanuatu flies compounded the problem; they approach cuts and scratches on human flesh with an all-you-can-eat buffet frenzy. Bandages fail to deter them;

they swarm over wound coverings and try to crawl underneath. My coworkers were unfazed by this. If *I* glanced down at a bandaged cut on my leg, however, to find a herd of large black flies struggling to burrow their way underneath my Band-Aid and into my flesh, I would frantically swat at them and then wrap my injury in duct tape.

The extent of Mike's injury left him with more than just flies to worry about. Medical staff treated him, but warned that if the condition worsened, he would be taken off the job and flown back to the States.

It was a typically gorgeous afternoon on Efaté when I headed toward one of our trailer-turned-offices. Three wooden steps led from the ground to the door. As my right foot came down on the first step, it trembled and a shudder swept through the entire trailer.

"Crap," I muttered, "I'm getting fat."

The trembling continued and grew and I knew that, despite whatever weight had recently attached to my buttocks, I did not yet have the power to make the earth shake. I looked around the job site, littered with temporary structures of little foundation. I didn't know what to do. During the six years that Mike and I lived in the San Francisco Bay Area, I had happily managed to sleep through a multitude of earthquakes.

I'd always thought that in such a situation I'd display clarity of thought and maybe a little bravery. Instead, my mind turned to mush and my spine followed. I should be with my husband, I thought, but then remembered that Mike was indefinitely confined to our hotel room, unable to walk and in hiding from the ravenous black flies.

I looked around for the nearest human, spotted one of the locals we'd hired who was moving with what seemed like a destination in mind and followed him. It turned out he was simply moving instinctively to evade the ground on which he stood, but you can't dodge an earthquake. We looked at each other with wide eyes and fearful grins. I wondered what his name was. If the ground opened up and swallowed the two of us with a belch of finality, I felt I should know the name of my unfortunate companion.

I was too scared for speech and apparently so was he, and the earthquake ended. As my coworkers emerged to giggle and discuss the excitement of the previous ten seconds, I thanked circumstance that I hadn't been in the port-a-potty at the time, then made my way there to determine how badly I'd wet myself.

A sign on the ladies' room door read: *Toilet blong ol woman.* I peeked over at the men's room: *Toilet blong ol man.* At first I took *ol* to mean *old,* as if these particular restrooms were reserved for elderly use. I pictured handrails and mechanical toilet seats to lower the user, then catapult them back to standing when finished. And then I wondered where they drew the age line. What constituted *ol*? Was there a particular number of years one had to have lived in order to make use of these facilities, like qualifying for a senior citizen's discount in the States? Of course, *ol* turned out to mean *only*; *Toilet blong ol (wo)man* was Bislama's elaborate distinction of men's and women's restrooms.

I would soon come to recognize *blong* as the most frequently employed word in Bislama. It can translate to *belong,* but also any other word signifying possession or a relationship. Instead of saying "his house," the Bislama speaker would say "house blong John."

I drove past the Pablik Laebri Blong Port Vila (Port Vila Public Library) and headed for the grocery store Au Bon Marche. On the other side of town was Au Bon Marche Nambatu. Figuring that Nambatu was someone's last name or something significant to Vanuatu culture, I didn't give it much thought. It only took two months of shopping at this store to figure out that Nambatu was, in fact Number Two.

My mission at Au Bon Marche involved purchasing Tuskers, the National beer (not to be confused with Kenya's beloved Tusker beer), the slogan for which is *Bia blong yumi* (It's our beer). I'd been charged with bringing beer to the crew. We'd reached the close of a long week and received a pass to indulge.

After consuming my share of Tuskers, I crossed the job site and felt the sudden rumble of another earthquake.

"Oh no," I whispered. My thoughts again turned to Mike. He was finally back on his feet only to be caught in what I suspected was the Mother of All Earthquakes. He stood fifty feet away, chatting and drinking with the rest of the crew. The earthquake hadn't yet registered with them, likely due to beer.

"Earthquake!" I yelled. They looked up, confronting me with calm but confused expressions.

Three ni-Van stood nearby, also unconcerned and drinking. They watched me run one way then the next shouting, "It's an earthquake! What do we do?"

"No, Amanda," one of them grabbed me by the arm. "Don't be scared. It's no earthquake." The rumbling continued; I didn't believe him. His companions were laughing at me. I didn't understand.

"It's only thunda chicken blong Jesus Christ," he explained.

I followed his arm up to the piercing blue heavens, where we watched a helicopter fly low over the treetops and out into the sky above the sea.

★

A.K. Turner has traveled the globe to research techniques on embarrassing herself in various cultures and languages. She now lives in Idaho where she created the radio program "The Writers' Block" for Radio Boise. She's the co-author of Drinking with Dead Women Writers *and the author of* This Little Piggy Went to the Liquor Store. *More of her work is available at AKTurner.com.*

LEIGH NANNINI

Motorcycle Mama

The joy of letting go, and holding on.

I WAS EIGHT WHEN I GOT MY FIRST ALL TERRAIN VEHICLE (ATV). It was red, shiny, and so advanced that I needed to shift gears (which I made sure to do with gusto). The machine's metallic intestines were exposed and the exhaust pipe constantly burned my calves. The clementine-sized blisters were nothing a pair of plastic cowgirl boots from Wal-Mart couldn't fix.

In no time, I deemed myself and demanded others call me "Motorcycle Mama." Unfortunately, my title came crashing down quickly. The faux-wood heel of my right boot fell off among the rotten fruit in the plum orchards and I was forced to walk like a carousel horse, slowing maneuvering up and down; faster if I was excited.

My friend Kristin didn't care about my lack of proper footwear and was a loyal passenger, clutching my abdomen as I pushed the throttle as far as it would go. We'd dig out empty plastic water bottles from the recycling bin, unscrew the caps, and hold them open in the wind, trying to catch cicadas. We'd fill the under seat compartment with freshly picked raspberries, park the machine, then devour the slightly-smelling-like-gasoline-exhaust fruit.

After I turned sixteen, the cherry bomb Kawasaki could no longer fulfill my desires to explore the world. It wasn't as cool as a vehicle that required an actual drivers license. I retired the machine to my father's stone quarry, to be used as a courtesy vehicle.

I never looked back. Wasn't that what my ATV taught me—to look onward. To see what was ahead, under the overgrown grass. To see if this journey had any visible speed bumps?

Then, almost twenty-four hours after we said "I do," my husband and I landed on a 100-step cement staircase in Santorini, Greece, where tan men wearing white linen uniforms and white-framed sunglasses painted our hotel's already-white exterior bright white.

"Are your legs shaking," I asked Oscar when we finally arrived in our cave-like suite appropriate for all types of romantic encounters. My thighs felt like jelly. "I mean, I'm a certified pilates instructor. I'm in shape. The best shape of my life." I caressed my rear end, as if to say, look, this thing is rock hard.

"It's just these stairs . . . they're so steep and there's so many," I continued.

As we dipped zucchini fritters in tzatziki under the umbrellas on the beach, the faint noise of ATV engines roared in the background. I half expected to hear crashing plates and the guttural "OPA," so I was slightly disappointed and ignored the revving of motors.

As we ate sticky Greek donuts on the side of a cobblestone street, I rolled my eyes at the tourists flying by on four-wheelers smaller than my seven-year-old nephew's.

It seemed like everywhere we turned, the island was infiltrated with these multi-colored ATVs.

"They look like idiots, in their helmets and the big RENT ME sticker plastered on the side of their new toys," I said to Oscar about the tourists flying by. "They are screaming ignorant vacationer. No Greek people ride those things."

"Actually, I think it's pretty cool," he said. The romantic honeymoon soundtrack playing in my mind stopped. "When else would you be able to ride one of those on city streets? And it'll certainly help with all of the stair climbing. You're always complaining about your burning thighs. I think we should do it."

Deep down, this was exactly what I was afraid of. Oscar, who grew up in Venezuela, had a very different upbringing than I did. While I was riding my go-carts and helping my dad dig dirt on an excavator, he was learning how to program a computer to say "hello." I had gotten the crazy ATV riding out of my system early on.

"Well, my body can handle the stairs," I said. "I don't want to rent one and look stupid."

"I do."

Perhaps it was the fact that we had just said those words so lovingly to each other in front of our friends and family. Perhaps it was something inside of me that wanted him to have that feeling I had as a kid. That feeling of being free, of having the wind blow through your hair at excessive speeds.

Whatever it was, I caved and we soon found ourselves at the rental shop, forking over Oscar's New York license. The Greek sales associate was stereotypically blasé, and I couldn't help but check my sunburn in the reflection of his Raybans.

Five minutes later, we strapped on bright orange salad-bowl-style helmets and were out the door. The gas tank was on empty (which I felt to be a bad omen), so we stopped at a gas station. Oscar had no shame as he pumped fuel into our ride. He smiled, giddy with excitement, and proudly wore his helmet into the building to pay. I stared down, diverting eye contact with the drivers waiting behind us. When was it socially acceptable to take this treacherous looking helmet off?

Once refueled, Oscar pushed the 100-horsepower engine as far as it could go. It wasn't nearly as fast as my Kawasaki, and oftentimes we had to wave of our arms, without turning around, for cars to pass us. Going downhill, we both leaned forward, hunched over, to make sure we were as aerodynamic as possible. But it didn't make a difference. This thing was slow.

Within an hour, we found ourselves at the top of a mountain, looking down on the classically beautiful white buildings. I forgot I was wearing a helmet and attempted to kiss Oscar, only to have my visor poke his eye. After a quick check to make sure his eyeball was still intact, that free feeling came back to me.

I turned to Oscar and whispered, "I'm your Motorcycle Mama now."

★

Leigh Nannini lives in the Hudson Valley region of New York where she works at the family business, a stone quarry. Similarities between the Nannini family, a stone quarry. Similarities between her life and that of Pebbles Flintstone are abundant. Despite her resistance, Leigh still finds herself in the passenger's seat of various forms of tourist-only transportation: camels in Giza, cable cars in Hong Kong, and tuk-tuks in Bangkok. She comes to terms with this.

NICO CRISAFULLI

An Indian Wedding Nothing Like the Movies

*The honor of your presence is requested
at the Whisky A Go-Go.*

I'LL BE THE FIRST TO ADMIT, MY PERCEPTIONS OF TRADITIONAL
Indian weddings came mostly by way of movies I'd seen.
And in these movies there were always scenes of wonder, glittering nose rings, austere ceremony, even the god-
damn Holy Fire ritual. I figured my first Indian wedding
would have whooping from the multitudes, all peacock-
ing around in perfect Bollywood cinematography. There
would be monkeys in hats, a fish on a tray, and young
couples that barely knew each other.

Sadly, my first Indian wedding had none of these things.
Mine was what you might call a catastrophe. Mine saw me
sitting in a grim little circle of teenage boys, cutting plastic
cups of cheap whiskey with water from a pipe sticking out
of a bare concrete embankment.

It was Varanasi in Spring. And like some do, I'd signed
up for a sunrise boat ride down the Ganges. Varanasi. A

city whose river is far holier than your city's river and doesn't even care, a city whose skyline looked like Shiva's baby boy had spilled its bag of toy blocks all over the landscape and left them there for a thousand years. It was a destination I'd been greatly looking forward to, perhaps for no other reason than to see what all the fuss was about, to peer into the arcane depths of the Mother Ganges and feel the mystical covenant that keeps Indians coming in droves to wash and immerse themselves in water that with one sip might kill any single one of them. I wanted to make sure those amoebic currents had a level of sanctity to negate the painfully scientific facts I knew about it—the jets of human sewage that gutted into the water just upstream from where the masses dunked their heads, prayed to Shiva, and felt shivers of his spirit enter their bodies. I'd heard of its fecal count, and it wasn't good. On the river, I could see how that foul effluence tainted its water jet black, see the detritus of a million purges, but I was sure I could overlook all that if I just squinted hard enough.

There were four other people who signed up for the tour that morning along with me, all of whom were no less than fifteen minutes late in coming down. Needless to say, my blood boiled. I wanted them hurt. I wanted to wave my itinerary in their faces and tell them this was my sunrise morning and not to fuck it up! But as is the irony of angry men, the world's ill manners embarrassed me with kindness. I was sitting with the young tour leader, Ravi, at a hard plastic table on the guesthouse patio, fantastically groggy, but excited about the idea of seeing some of the world's most pristine activity from the comfort of a painfully adorable wooden boat. Through the pre-dawn hum, I heard Ravi engaging me with small talk.

"Many pilgrims are coming here to bathe in the Ganga. It is a very pious river."

"Yes," I said. "I'm looking forward to the sunrise."

"You know," he said quite matter-of-factly, "tonight I am being married."

"How's that?"

"Today is my wedding day."

"Er, you . . . Are you serious?" I croaked, stopping short of asking just what he was thinking working on his wedding day. Instead he read the incredulousness on my face and offered his open palm as evidence. It was decorated to the wrist with the swirling henna curlicues indicative to, sure enough, an Indian wedding. I almost cried.

That night he was to marry his bride, and the most wonderful day in his life started with me, a jaded American forty-something who hadn't washed his underwear in a week. I wanted to hug him.

Things changed quickly when I realized he was asking if I would please do him the honor of joining him that night at the wedding. And would eight o'clock be okay?

I stiffened with panic.

Tonight? Me? Who was I even? I had nothing to wear! Certainly no English would be spoken. But most importantly, what would I wear? My formal attire at that point of my travels consisted of exactly one pair of long pants and one shirt with a collar, and those were, shall we say, vastly unbefitting of a fine occasion. I was sure there was a giant curry stain on the thigh and who knew how much cow shit my butt had been privy to over the previous weeks. Screw it, I thought. I'd be going to that wedding, cow shit and curry notwithstanding.

That night, I made it back to the guesthouse at exactly ten minutes to eight. Six minutes to shower and four-and-a-half minutes to deal with the pant leg, and I was out the door. Only to find myself waiting over an hour in the guesthouse kitchen with nothing to do but stand around with two of Ravi's young friends, Manu and Prem,

steamrolled by an encouragingly offered and unceremoni-
ously quaffed bottle Officer's Choice whiskey.

It was approaching 9:30 when we finally and for no
evident reason left that drinky kitchen. The boys moved
me quickly out of the guesthouse and through the narrow
alleys with their arms woven through mine, whisking me
away to an event utterly unsuited to my rapid descent into
intoxication.

Very soon thereafter I was being placed at a feast.
Roughly 150 wedding guests were gathered together eating, barely speaking, hungry teeth devouring a seemingly
endless supply of food. Through no fault of my own I
was stuffed full of India's finest fare: poori, naan, samosas,
spoonfuls of saag, ladles of dahl—dinner I would've loved
to enjoy had I not been a tipsy and altogether inappropriate mess. I'd wanted just one damn moment to enjoy
a plate before another load of fluffy bread and chickpeas
was placed before me. It seemed the boys were intent on
making me puke. They dropped dish after dish on the
table, only to take them away half-eaten, and replaced with
another even more exotic and unidentifiable serving.

By this time the three boys around me had turned into
six, all grinning the most impish Indian grins, impossibly
white teeth shining at me, giggling as they stuffed me like
a prized turkey.

Somehow the dining portion revolved to a close. But
before I could say "so where's the happy couple," I was
being led again by the elbows out of the banquet area, the
two previous armholders now a half-dozen hands on my
shoulders and back, tittering loudly, scurrying me toward
a shadowy section of ghats fifty meters away, down twenty
steps toward the murky waterline, a hundred nautical miles
from my comfort zone. Manu and Prem, who had recently
vanished, returned with another bottle of Officer's Choice
whiskey. Thin plastic cups were distributed to each of our

now group of seven, which at my initial refusal, and their subsequent insistence, were filled deep.

Back in the kitchen we were cutting our whiskey with splashes of Limca soda. There on the ghat there was no Limca, only a thin line of water trickling out of a pipe sticking brazenly out of the concrete. The kids were busy cutting their own cups with the pipewater, mine following soon after. Was it even potable? I couldn't say. The rust told me otherwise but it didn't seem to matter to them in the slightest.

They cheerfully diluted my hard alcohol with pipewater that likely proffered a hundred billion harbingers of toilet Hell. I was at a loss. My drunkard's decision however was to drink it down and pray to the Lord God to assist in any future bathroom duties.

The night completely bypassed the dancing, bypassed the revelry and the tossing of marigold petals—in other words, bypassed all the fun. Gone was any donning of saffron turbans and the carrying of fish on silver trays. What happed next was the blatant dismissal of everything I had up until that moment expected from an Indian wedding, because Manu, the unmistakable alpha dog of our little group, decided that my now prodigious levels of intoxication were better suited to my guesthouse bedroom than the wedding—it was his fault!—and he ordered me taken home.

My supplications to speak with the groom were heard however and I was led back into the wedding party fray. There was a beehive of activity orbiting the bride and groom, a zoo of fawning and petting and flashbulb-sparkling cholis. Through a tilting haze I zeroed in on Ravi. He looked weary but fine in a perfectly pressed, richly embroidered wedding *sherwani*, standing next to what I assumed to be a flange of family members. I elbowed my way to him.

I remember quite the opposite of lucidly bowing my head, squashing my palms together and gushing Namastes and thank yous and I'm totally honored to be heres to any and every nearby wedding party member, effectively bullet-holing the room's sing song Hindi with a tawdry American obsequiousness. I also hardly remember my other embarrassing attempts at chivalry (did I really kiss the hand of the bride? Did I *do* that?). I soon noticed Manu approaching, parting the ocean of awkwardness.

Like a dog urging its master to take it outside, Manu's hand gently pressed at my elbow. The pressing soon became a pulling, but not before I felt it a good idea to wrap my arms around the mother of the bride in a boozy embrace, whereupon the pulling became a desperate yank punctuated with a solid, "*We go* now, *Baba!*"

Later, as the whisky curtain rose to illuminate the evening's events, I considered my night. I thought of how its moments played out like the images on a Bollywood screen, but nothing at all like the movies, my own sequel to someone else's lucky day. And Varanasi to me would be defined by it, not the by the mystical ceremonies executed under bedazzled skies, but by the bottoms of alcohol cups as they shaped the very memories I would eventually come to laugh at. It wasn't my idea of a holy wedding in a spiritual city, but it would have to do. It was all I had.

★

Nico's perspective of the world all but reversed upon visiting India for the first time in 2011, his respect for cows, spicy chai, and modern plumbing suddenly elevated. He now lives with his wife and young son along the shores of the San Francisco Bay, but promises an imminent return to India.

Ciao Bella

The ying-yang of adoration: damned if you do and damned if you don't.

WHEN MY MOTHER TURNED FIFTY, WE DECIDED IT WAS TIME she traveled. Aside from a few quick trips over the Mexican border, she'd never left the United States. She wanted to go some place clean—yet lively, cultural—but not overly foreign. We decided on Italy.

Only one thing worried her. *Watch out for the men,* a few people warned. *They are aggressive, will grope you, and make lewd comments—ESPECIALLY since you are blondes. Italian men love blondes.*

At fifty, my mom was quite good-looking and walking down the street together we accrued roughly about the same amount of male attention. She had a nice figure, beautiful face, and stylish clothes. I was less kempt, but at twenty-four had sea-white hair that flowed all the way down to my waist.

We brainstormed. What could we do to fend off the unwanted advances? Tying up our hair or hiding it beneath a hat was an option, but seemed too oppressive. So instead, we prepared what we would say in response and honed our snide looks. If an Italian man approached us with a dramatic proclamation of love, we knew exactly what we'd say: *I like your approach, now let's see your departure.*

Or were he to say something like *I know how to please a woman,* we would say, *Then please leave us alone.*

And reserved for the lewdest offenders: *Sorry, we don't date outside our species.*

Mom decided that instead of hotels, we would stay in the convents with the Holy Sisters—far, far away from the machismo of Italy's streets. We would be fine.

Should we bring pepper spray? My mother fretted. I laughed, but she was serious.

We started our tour of Italy in Venice, riding gondolas down the waterways and wandering the cobblestone streets. We were so awed by the beauty of the city that we forgot all about the perils of Italian men. We were too busy dining on pasta e fagioli, drinking the house wine, and blowing cigarette smoke over our shoulders. We spent a morning loitering in the Piazza San Marco where I fed what seemed like a thousand pigeons. One late afternoon, we strolled under the lines of clean laundry fluttering in the Venetian breeze.

Florence was next and we loved the bridges, walking the length of Ponte Vecchio back and forth a dozen times. We toured Galleria dell' Academia, eyeing the perfection of Michelangelo's David, and almost blushing at his beauty. So far, all was going well. Days had gone by, and not a single Italian man had leered. We hadn't even heard a *Ciao bella!* Mom began to relax.

Days peeled away in Lucca next. Each morning we rented bicycles and rode around the wall surrounding the town. We spent days drinking cappuccino and looking at clothing and ceramics. On Mom's birthday, I decorated her bike in crepe paper and loaded the basket with cakes and presents. We rode around the wall, parked our bikes, and celebrated at a picnic table. *Happy fiftieth Mom,* I said, lighting the candles.

On the way to Rome we put our guards back up. Rome would be the surely be the epicenter of unwanted catcalls and groping. We set stern expressions, ready to admonish any Georgio or Piero who got out of line.

Once in the city, we boarded a packed bus to the Sistine Chapel. *Watch it,* mom said as we squeezed in and stood pelvis-to-pelvis with a crowd of Italian men. We exchanged worried glances the whole ride, but once again nothing happened. As we entered the chapel, I became aware of a gnawing question, which I kept to myself. *Where were all the aggressive Italian men?* I wondered. *Was there something wrong with us?*

Not ten minutes later, a young Italian man in glasses and too-short pants approached us with a look of faint desire. Mom braced. *Finally,* I sighed. He addressed my mother with the utmost politeness, a pure gentleman: *Your daughter is beautiful. Can I ask your permission to take her on a date?*

A few days later, we boarded a train to Milan where we'd catch our flight back to the U.S. Mom must have been feeling a bit desperate because she stood close to the conductor and flirted with him. By the time the train pulled into Milan, she'd secured us a date. *He has a friend,* she whispered. We followed him off the train, and he led us to the employee cafeteria where his friend, a fifty-something named Giovanni, waited. We split a bag of chips four ways.

All that worry and preparation and not a single catcall. We didn't even get to use the lines we'd rehearsed so studiously. My mother and I left Italy deeply offended.

Years have passed since our trip to Italy, and on some level I still haven't forgotten the wounding indifference of Italy's men. But recently, I've been spending my mornings in a café in Sausalito, California. The place is frequented by Italians and each morning as I pass the sidewalk tables

I hear a chorus of *Ciao Bella,* and *Beautiful Smile.* When I step to the cream counter with my coffee, the men glance up from their newspapers, and my ego swells like a popover. It's as if all the ogling men that were supposed to be in Italy had gathered in this small Sausalito café.

One morning, I was standing at the register paying for my espresso. An older Italian man was at a table behind me, his eyes about level with my buttocks.

Ciao Bella, he said. I braced and returned a stiff *Hi.*

How are you? he asked.

Fine. You?

Well . . . I love this point of view he answered. His watery eyes leered at the back of my jeans.

I felt heat rise under my shirt. *How inappropriate* I gasped. *How politically incorrect.* Where was this guy in Italy, I wondered, when I was prepared, guarded, and equipped. Now, standing there at the counter, I couldn't remember a single one of the comebacks my mom and I had prepared. So I turned and said the first thing that came to mind:

Thanks.

★

Christina Ammon is a travel writer with work published in Orion Magazine, *the* San Francisco Chronicle, The Oregonian, Eating Well *and other publications. She is the winner of a gold SOLAS award for family travel and recipient of an Oregon Literary Arts award for creative nonfiction. She is currently traveling the world in a truck made of garbage. Visit her blog at www.vanabonds.com.*

KIM MANCE

Any Bears
Around Today?

She didn't anticipate becoming prey.

THERE IS NO ROAD TO CHURCHILL. TO REACH THIS COMMU-
nity of 900 on Hudson Bay in Manitoba, Canada, travelers
must fly, sail or ride a train. The nearest town is about 170
miles away. I made the forty-eight-hour rail journey from
Winnipeg, past prairie farms, through foggy forests, and
eventually over subarctic permafrost.

When the train finally eased into Churchill's station, I
had one thing on my mind: polar bears. It's the first thing
I think of when conjuring images of the Canadian north.
Having grown up in Colorado, where I was immersed in
adrenaline-inducing activities, I'm a sucker for adventure.
Combine that with the possibility of spotting a threatened
species in the wild and this, for me, was a trip I couldn't
resist.

I was soon jostling over rocks along a dirt road in an
enormous and boxy thirty-eight-passenger vehicle called
a "Tundra Buggy," outfitted with monster truck wheels
and rectangular sliding windows. Our guide, Dave, gave
riders a polar bear safety briefing as we ventured through

the wildlife preserve outside town. Polar bears are the world's largest carnivorous land mammals and nearly 1,000 of them are found in the region, so I listened more attentively than I do to, say, airline safety spiels. "Don't put your hands outside the windows," he warned. "Last year a guy wanted to get a better picture and snapped his fingers to get the bear's attention. The bear ripped his arm off."

Noted.

As our massive white buggy lumbered through muddy paths, Dave scanned the horizon. Suddenly, he pointed to a white dot about 200 yards across the boggy tundra.

"Look, over there," he yelled, "by the waterfront!"

Sure enough, a polar bear lazily stretched out on its back, at the edge of the Hudson's lapping waves. It rolled over and plunked a paw on its brown stony bed, unaware of the thrill it was providing us. I stood on the buggy's back deck watching through binoculars, marveling at each rise and fall of the bear's chest as it breathed in crisp, cool air.

On the way back to Churchill, Dave offered more warnings, urging us to stay away from side streets in town and areas with trash cans—and to avoid sitting on the bay-side boulders because bears could be sleeping under them. "Don't worry, the twenty-four-hour Bear Patrol will send off 'bear shot' warnings to try and keep them away," Dave said. "If one gets into town and you're not near your hotel the patrol truck will come by and pick you up."

The population of Churchill swells with visitors each year as bear season draws near, but I began to understand that there was more to my visit than just my hunt for bear sightings. I'd come to the bears' home. And I was prey.

I felt a palpable awareness of the bears. In a local diner, rather than remarking on the weather or sports scores, friends greeted each other with the question, "Any bears around today?"

Each person I met added his or her own advice on how to handle a bear confrontation. Flipping his monocle down over a pair of glasses, eighty-year-old town jeweler Ed admonished, "If you see one, stand completely still. They can't see very well, so if you don't move at all you have a better chance of not being noticed."

Walking to dinner, I found my eyes darting left and right—not in search of traffic, but bears. Simply crossing the road to the edge of town was an adventure. "Oh crap, what is that?" I said to myself. And just as I was about to run, er, stand completely still, it was revealed to be only a white minivan on the horizon. Whew.

At dusk one night (the sun sets late in the subarctic summer), the center of town was quiet except for laughter and chatter wafting from a pub called Tundra. Inside, it was packed with beer-drinking Churchill residents and I soon met a bearded man in his 20s named Chris Cooke, or "Cookie," as others around the table called him. He smiled and rolled his eyes but answered my questions about growing up around bears. Cookie spoke of close encounters, learning to stay aware, and how many Churchillians had been killed before the Bear Patrol was established in the 1980s (the last one being a guy who fell asleep on his porch in '82 and was eaten). Cookie often kept a rifle handy, but he said being around the bears was now second nature.

After a few drinks, I asked if he'd ever had to shoot at a bear. His eyes fell and his shoulders slumped; Cookie grabbed his bottle of beer and described the time a bear unexpectedly showed up in his backyard, blocking the path between him and his house. "I didn't have a choice," Cookie said. "He began charging me."

Lifting his hand to his shoulder, Cookie mimicked the bear stopping its charge and grasping a bloody wound. "People don't think of the bears having a shoulder, just like we do," he said. "It still haunts me, him grabbing it when I shot him. We all live up here together, us and the bears."

All in all, I spotted eighteen polar bears during my weeklong stay. But as it turned out, the bears weren't the highlight of the trip. It was the jovial and friendly people who choose to weather the elements and live in this unforgiving environment a world away from everyone else—who commute by exceedingly slow trains to shop for clothes or consult with a medical specialist. These residents happily give bear safety advice to visitors. They are people who live an adventure every day and put my own adventures to shame.

By my last day I'd become more confident walking the streets, just as the town began to buzz with news that the Northern Lights would appear that night.

As I craned my neck at 2 A.M., mesmerized by the presence of the fabled Aurora Borealis, a custodian came out of a nearby building and began staring up alongside me. The ethereal greenish mass swirled above. Though I've never been one to make small talk about weather, this magical phenomenon tempted me to break the silence and ask if he, too, thought it was amazing, even though he lived here.

But then, pulling a cigarette from his mouth, he spoke first.

"Any bears around tonight?" he asked.

★

Kim Mance is a travel writer and TV host based in Brooklyn. She is a contributing blogger to Conde Nast Traveler's website, and has written and blogged for outlets like Marie Claire, World Hum, *and* Huffington Post. *Kim is also editor of GoGalavanting.com.*

LAUREN QUINN

Packaged in Puerto

A maverick discovers the great equalizer—
the swim-up bar.

IT WASN'T THE HUMIDITY THAT HAD CRUSHED OUR SPIRITS. It wasn't the trendy juice bars, dodgy tattoo shops or trinket stores selling frayed ponchos and luchador masks. It was the men of Puerto Vallarta that had gotten us down. Their barrage of hoots, honks, hollers, kissing noises, and dramatic, teeth-sucking inhalations had sent us over the edge.

Melissa was the first to crack. "The next motherfucker to hassle us," she declared, "is getting it right back."

Sure enough, twenty seconds later, a car passed, its driver leaning half his torso out of the unrolled window in order to better look at us. Melissa made kissey noises and wiggled her fingers at him in a ball-fondling motion.

Confusion and disappointment quaked across the driver's face as he sped away.

"You asshole," Georgina said to Melissa. "That was a cab driver."

Things were not going well for us in Puerto Vallarta. To be fair, we hadn't done our research. My three girl-friends and I had just spent a week in the Michoacán town Pátzcuaro, home to one of the most traditional Dia de los Muertos celebrations in Mexico. We'd shopped the craft market for Catrina dolls, eaten cabeza tacos at street stalls, spent a night with local families in a candle-lit, altar-adorned cemetery. Amidst the celebrations, our tattoos, piercings and gender had gone largely unnoticed—who cares about a bunch of rock-and-roll white girls when there's sugar skulls to be eaten?

Experiencing authentic, traditional culture with locals is great, but we were still in Mexico—it seemed a waste to come all that way and not get in a few good beach days. So we'd chosen the closest, most accessible sun-and-sand destination from land-locked Pátzcuaro; one day of dubbed movies on rattling buses and we arrived in Puerto Vallarta.

Had we done our homework, the sudden demographic shift wouldn't have been such a shock. In contrast to Pátzcuaro—as difficult to reach as it was to pronounce—Puerto Vallarta was thoroughly on the tourist path. Direct flights from the U.S. soared in daily, and cruise ships docked regularly, spilling out hoards of people who weren't seeking traditional culture with locals—they wanted a cheap, easy vacation. And maybe a smoothie.

We traversed sidewalks lined with English-language signs, swarmed with the running shoes, khaki shorts and baseball caps of Middle America, under a battery of verbal assault from what seemed every man in Mexico. Sometimes they opted to translate their solicitations: "*Guapa*, you want sex?" In Puerto Vallarta's touristy center, not even the catcalls were 100 percent authentic.

We'd scoffed at the all-inclusive resorts we'd passed on the way from the bus station. We were independent travelers—private beaches, piped-in music, and watery margaritas weren't our scene. But one day spent wandering Puerto Vallarta, and one unsuspecting cabbie harassed, and we wanted in.

Alicia scoured our Lonely Planet and found a resort that purportedly offered day passes. We piled in a cab and headed out of central Puerto Vallarta, through wide avenues lined with strip malls and corporate chains: Pizza Hut, Starbucks, OfficeMax, Outback Steakhouse. It felt more like an American suburb than a Mexican vacation paradise.

We stepped out of the cab onto a deserted, windy sidewalk, and scurried up the manicured walkway to the resort's foyer. Our sneakers squeaked across the polished floor as we approached the reception desk.

A woman in an ill-fitting navy blazer looked out from under her crow's feet at us. "Yessss," she said slowly.

"*Hola*," I began confidently. "*Queremos comprar* . . . ." I trailed off, my Spanish vocabulary extinguished. I hung my head and whispered: "day passes."

"$25 each." The receptionist answered in English. And in dollars.

"Dude," Georgina hissed, "the guidebook said it was only ten bucks."

I smiled an impotent smile, leaned in. "*Y cuantos para cuatro?*"—my Spanish reignited.

The receptionist blinked once, twice, then answered, "$100 for four. No discount."

We held a hush-voiced meeting, in which it was agreed that a fee equal to a night in our hotel room was too high. We'd suck it up, pay for a taxi back into town, and suffer through the assault of catcalls on the city beach. Or stay in the hotel room with the shades drawn.

Defeated, sweaty, and a bit annoyed, we wandered towards the sidewalk. A groundskeeper in a little golf buggy slowed as he passed. "*Hola!*" he exclaimed merrily. "*Perdidas?* Are you lost?"

"Oh, we're just trying to catch a cab," Alicia explained.

"You're not going to the pools?" he asked incredulously, raising eyebrows that looked like spider's legs. "Perfect day."

"No," we chorused sadly.

"But you are from the cruise ship, yeees?" he nodded to the gray monstrosity docked in the distance, visible between the cement towers of oceanfront hotels. The way he elongated the "yes" inspired me to nod vaguely.

"And you lost your wrist bands. Is O.K. Get on, I will take you to the pools."

We didn't wait for further explanation or invitation. We leapt on the little white go-cart.

As we toddled through the generic shrubbery and 70s block buildings of the resort, we pieced it together: a cruise ship had docked for the day and its guests were given complimentary day passes to the resort. Our driver, pausing now to beep and wave at a fellow employee, had for some reason decided to "confuse" us with cruisers.

We didn't care what had inspired him, or how much the surroundings looked like a cross between a retirement community and a failed attempt at a Club Med commercial. It was peaceful, free of honks and whistles. We chatted idly with our benefactor-cum-smuggler about California and where his relatives lived as we made our way through the complex.

We pulled up behind a cluster of thatched umbrellas. "The pools are there," he pointed. Then, with an assuring nod, "Is O.K. you lost your wrist bands."

We hopped off the buggy, exchanging back-pats and high-fives; forever the waitress, I slipped the driver a sizable peso note as I shook his hand. He waved, and trundled off into the landscaped distance.

I felt a twist in my stomach as we surveyed the pools. I was afraid of being caught—bum-rushed, I imagined, by a SWAT team of hotel management. With our sleeves of tattoos, dyed hair and septum piercings, we'd surely stand out among the suburban-American resort-goers.

But I was equally afraid of being mistaken for one of them.

I led the way through a maze of lounge chairs, arm floaties and sunburns. Women in one-pieces, hats over their faces, lay napping in the sun. A balding man with a potbelly splashed with a child, wearing those silly, reptilian swim shoes. Two boys with spiky, frost-tipped hair flexed their adolescent pecs at eyelash-batting female counterparts.

No one paid us any mind.

We plopped our bags down next to a couple of weathered chairs and began rubbing white sunscreen into multicolored skin. Instead of a chorus of whistles and honks, Top 20 hits from the last twenty years pumped out of stereo speakers hung from poles and fashioned to resemble coconuts. It was the same basic soundtrack of every middle school dance I'd gone to, and I felt, in that moment, just about as awkward.

Ace of Base blared out suddenly over the speakers. "Ooh, this is my song!" Melissa cried sarcastically. She began lip-synching and shaking her tiny hips in a Macarena-style fashion to "I Saw The Sign."

We entered the pool—either by gingerly sliding (me) or cannon-balling (Melissa)—and began wading through the bath-water-warm construction of bridges, slides and fountains that dripped with children's limbs.

And then we saw it.

Or Alicia saw it. Her neck did a whip-lash double-take and she blurted out a pointed, "Oh hell no."

We followed her stare. There, like a yeti espied in its native habitat, was a swim-up bar.

"I didn't know those actually existed!" I cried.

We floated up to the thatched roof and blinking lights of the bar, half-giggly, half-amazed. We soon had a row of tall, neon margarita slushies adorned with twisty straws and paper umbrellas before us.

"Nice tattoo," a sun-spotted woman beside us said. She pointed to the laughing skeleton across my chest. "It's a Posada calavera?"

I grinned. "Yes!" Then, with a sly smile, "A lot of people think it's a Grateful Dead tattoo. In the States, at least."

The woman laughed and shook her Golden-Girls 'fro. "Well, we *are* in Mexico."

She was right. It may have been the Chevy's of beach resorts, but we were still in Mexico.

She offered to take our picture—four girls embracing, holding out Slurpie-colored drinks in waist-deep pool water. It was a simple gesture between tourists, and in that moment, I didn't feel Other Than. I didn't feel like The Intrepid Independent Traveler, not The Ugly American, nor The Feminist Gringa Being Harassed. I had nothing to prove and no one else to be.

Who cares about being the rock n roll white girl when there's a swimming pool and cheap drinks to be had?

And then a Mariah Carey Christmas song came on.

★

Lauren Quinn is a writer from Oakland, California. Her work has appeared in 7x7, the San Francisco Chronicle, *and on websites such as* World Hum, Matador, *and the* Huffington Post. *She writes the blog Lonely Girl Travels and is currently living in Phnom Penh, Cambodia.*

Turkish Foreplay

The consequences of riding shotgun.

"Where are you from?" the young man asked. He adjusted the rear view mirror in time to witness me reach for the tissues in my purse.

"San Francisco . . . California," I replied to a mop of thick black curls and the big brown eyes in the mirror, my view of the driver from the back seat of the car. My voice came out as a squeak. I'd been feeling sorry for myself and verged on tears.

Twenty-four hours without sleep, four airports, three flights, a handful of pitiful meals, who knew how many thousands of miles, and I'd arrived in Turkey without luggage. I tried not to be a baby about it. People deal with lost luggage all the time. But still, I felt an overwhelming amount of defeat. In two days, I was to leave Bodrum's harbor aboard a boat for a weeklong excursion on the Aegean Sea with ten women I didn't know.

Traveling alone, I couldn't share the burden of missing luggage and worried I'd be boarding that boat with nothing but a toothbrush in my back pocket. There was hardly any time to shop, and purchasing a week's supply of sailing attire felt daunting—I have a hard enough time shopping at home. So I wasn't feeling talkative in the car on the way to Bodrum, yet the driver persisted in a thick, brawny accent—a contrast to the soft manner in which he spoke.

"California," he parroted, and then asked another question.

"I'm sorry, can you repeat that?"

"What do you do?" he asked again.

"I'm a designer. Websites mostly."

"Oh, websites."

After a bit of strained silence, he asked another question, barely audible.

"Can you repeat that?" I leaned closer to the front seat to hear better, but that didn't help. He'd had to ask the question several more times, and with each utterance, I leaned in closer and closer.

"How long you stay?" he stammered.

"Only two nights in Bodrum. Then I'm going on a gull-et for a week with a group of writers."

"Gull-et?" he asked, perplexed.

"You know, a traditional Turkish boat. Is that the wrong pronunciation?" I felt a little embarrassed.

"Goo-let," he replied.

The driver seemed especially interested in getting to know me. I assumed his attempts at small talk were to distract me from my visible anxiety. He'd had to wait for me outside the airport for an hour as I ran from one baggage carousel to another. I saw him peering in at me, face pressed against the window with cupped hands, as the hazard lights on his car blinked on and off in the passenger pickup zone while I filled out a lost luggage report. One minute! I mimed with my index finger. He looked impatient, and I didn't want him to leave without me. There were no other taxis going to Bodrum at that late hour; I'd arranged the car service with my hotel before leaving San Francisco.

The driver pulled over at a gas station.

"Would you like water?" he asked.

"No thanks," I answered, mostly for having nothing smaller than a fifty lira bill—the equivalent of $40.

"I am going to have water . . . please, have water," he persisted with a smile.

"O.K., then. If it makes you happy." I waited in the car, impressed by Turkish hospitality.

The driver returned from the shop with two bottles, and before getting into the car, poked his head in my window to ask if I'd like to sit in the front seat.

A little strange, I thought. But then again, I know a lot of people hate feeling like a chauffeur, even though in essence, that was his job. I gathered my things and got into the front seat—I'd been leaning in so close, I might as well have been sitting there in the first place. Plus, I figured there might be better views from up there and perhaps I could stop asking the driver to repeat himself.

"What is your name?" he asked.

"Cheryn. And yours?"

"Ekmed," he replied, "How old are you?"

"Thirty-six. And you?"

"Twenty-five," Ekmed said. "You have nice eyes," he added after a moment.

"Thank you."

"Your boyfriend?" Ekmed asked, referring to the ring on my left hand.

"Yes."

"Where is your boyfriend?" he wanted to know.

"He's at home."

"Is your boyfriend good?" Ekmed inquired.

I wasn't sure what he was asking, so I answered to cover all the bases, "Yes, he's very healthy and wishes he could be here, but since I'm here for a workshop with other writers, he would be bored. And he is a great guy all around. I am glad he is my boyfriend. Yes, he is good."

Then Ekmed waved his hand obliquely, saying, "This is good."

I thought perhaps he was referring to a scenic view—although it was pitch black outside—or a tasty restaurant nestled in a cluster of buildings I could make out on the shore that ran parallel to the highway.

I asked, "It's good? What is good?"

"This," Ekmed replied, again waving his hand in a non-directional way that gave me the feeling he was referring to the interchange between us. Surely he could not have meant our conversation, difficult and limited as it was. But with English not being his native tongue, nor a fluent foreign tongue, perhaps it was a good conversation in his view, all things considered.

". . . . Turkish boyfriend?" Ekmed asked.

"I'm sorry, I don't understand what you mean," I replied, fearing I did.

". . . . Turkish boyfriend?" he repeated.

The thought dawned on me that he was asking if I'd like a Turkish boyfriend, but I didn't want to respond to that sort of question just in case he wasn't. I didn't want to look presumptuous or interested or put the idea in his head if it hadn't been there already.

"My boyfriend is not Turkish," I said, to be on the safe side.

He accepted this as an answer, and—I presume—understanding he would have to change tactics, Ekmed put his hand out, palm up, and looked at me with an expectant expression.

"What?" I asked.

Ekmed grabbed my hand and held it in his, intimately, with fingers interlaced. There we were, driving down a deserted dark highway, halfway to Bodrum, holding hands like teenagers on a first date. I had to suppress a giggle as I thought to myself, somewhat flattered by his attention, *really?!* And then I began to worry, *is this that moment before things go really, really wrong for the woman traveling alone?* We were in the middle of nowhere. All I could see were the black silhouettes of trees whizzing by the window and a few feet of pavement in front of us, lit by the car's headlamps.

"I think you should drive with both hands," I said, extricating my hand while placing his back on the wheel.

Ekmed looked a little wounded, a tad embarrassed, but not enough to refrain from asking for a kiss while pointing at a place on his clean-shaven cheek very, very close to a pair of puckering lips.

"I cannot kiss you," I told him, "Remember? I have a boyfriend."

"But vacation is for relaxing," Ekmed seemed honestly confused.

"You're right," I said, measuring my words carefully, "and all I want to do right now is *sleep.*"

There was silence after this. Awkward silence. But it was much better than awkward conversation and awkward come-ons. We arrived to the hotel and Ekmed politely walked me to the reception desk. Aside from being tired and irritable from all the hours of travel and the missing luggage, I was stunned at what had taken place. I couldn't stop wondering if this was what traveling solo is like. Thinking about previous trips with my boyfriend, he and Ekmed would be halfway to drinking buddies by now, and I'd have been ignored in the back seat.

Later at the hotel bar, I recounted my experience to the woman who organized the trip. She laughed and apologized for not warning me ahead of time; she'd been living in Turkey for a few years.

"Don't sit in the front of the taxi," she said, "it's a signal that you're interested in sex."

Apparently, Turkey is a destination for lonely women who arrive seeking love and *relaxation* in the arms of temporary vacation boyfriends. Sitting in the front seat of a car is Turkish foreplay.

A few weeks later, I again found myself in the back seat of a taxi on the way to the airport. My flight was leaving early, and I'd woken the driver at the taxi stand at 3:30 A.M. by knocking on the window of his car. On the way to the airport, I could see his drooping eyelids in the rear view mirror as his head bobbed to and fro with every bump in the pavement. He was dozing off at the wheel while speeding down the highway. I feared that should I talk to him, the driver would misconstrue my attention, but I feared more the ending of my life.

"Excuse me," I leaned in from the back seat, risking my betrothal to the Turkish driver, "what is your name?"

★

Cheryn Flanagan lives in Oakland, California, and spends most days thinking about digital interfaces and experience design. But she's happiest when able to leave the desk behind to explore the world with pen and camera. Her travel stories focus on personal quests, food history, and astronomical phenomena.

DAVID FARLEY

Monkeying around in Paris

An encounter with locals leads the author
to lose his monkey-mind.

A FEW FACTS ABOUT PARIS: MORE THAN SIX HUNDRED PEOPLE are sent to the hospital after slipping in dog poop each year. One thousand two hundred people who rode the Metro today, ended it without their wallet. And according to *Time Out Paris*, an estimated 100 lions, tigers, and panthers are kept as pets in the city's apartments. I had moved into a tiny ground-floor apartment on Rue des Pyramides, a baguette's throw from the Louvre. One day, when my landlord had dropped by to collect the rent, I mentioned the fact about the exotic, possibly man-eating animals living in Paris. "I believe it," she said, unfazed. "We French love animals."

If you believe that, here's another fact from my guidebook to twist your mind around: in the Paris suburb Aubervilliers, illegally imported apes have been trained to attack people—and to go for the face when they do. The Paris suburbs are not soccer mom safe havens like in the United States. In places like Aubervilliers, about five miles north of the city, ambulances won't even answer an emergency call unless accompanied by the police. This much could be true. But man-assaulting suburban apes just outside of Paris? I was doubtful.

I'd only been in Paris for a month, but the City of Light was already straining my eyes. I had to abandon the article I was writing about the myth of Parisian rudeness because, well, I had no evidence that it was a myth. My French was worse than I thought, as I was reminded just about every time I opened my mouth. And, given my limited budget, "eating out" mostly consisted of sitting on the banks of the Seine with a baguette and some cheese and a bottle of wine to wash it all down with.

One night, while doing just that, a man approached me trying to hock a French magazine about monkeys. In halting French I asked him if he'd heard of Aubervilliers and then pointed to the apes on the cover of his magazine while making the international "I'm going to tear your face off sign" with my hands. "Oh yes," he said with enthusiasm. "There are apes in Aubervilliers. But I'm not sure if you want to go there."

The next morning I was on the subway heading in the direction of Aubervilliers. Armed with only a return subway ticket hidden in my sock, I practiced a few phrases I had memorized for the occasion. The Aubervilliers stop was near the end of the line. As the train neared the northern border between Paris and its suburbs, ominous-sounding subway stations came and went: Crimee, Stalingrad. I then remembered a friend back in San Francisco warning me that the worst place I could go was the suburbs north of Paris. He had a Parisian friend who lived near there. Apparently, his friend once took a wrong turn on her scooter and ended up in a bad section. While stopped at a red light she was suddenly knocked to the ground.

Within seconds, her purse, jacket, shoes *and* scooter were out of sight.

When I walked up the steps from the subway, the streets of Aubervilliers looked surprisingly civil. There were no burning mattresses on the side of the street, no roving gangs stealing people's shoes and, unfortunately, no face-scraping wild apes. I walked around for fifteen minutes, looking into the plethora of seedy bars and cheap textile stores, hoping to get some clue about the apes—and also wondering if one might just run out of nowhere and jump on me. Finally, I wandered into a café where two rough-faced working-class men were drinking beer (it was 9:30 in the morning). I ordered a coffee, trying to give off a vibe that said I was meant to be there. In France, it's all about attitude.

I practiced my French ape-related phrases as I nursed my strong, surprisingly tasty coffee. Rain started to pour outside. After taking my final sip, I took a deep breath and made my way over to the two men who were talking about *futbol* in between swigs of beer. "*Excusez-moi, parlez-vous Anglais?*" I asked, hoping for a more beneficial exchange in my native language. The man closest to me briefly looked up from his beer, then looked at his friend. I waited five long seconds before asking again. Finally, he responded in French: "You want me to speak English?" His tone was more aggressive than curious. He covered his upper lip with his lower and shook his head slowly, still not looking at me. His friend muttered something indiscernible. By this point, both men and the bartender wore smirks, as if I were wearing a clown suit with a sign on it that said, "MONKEYS SUCK."

"O.K., I will speak French," I said, deliberately slow, hoping I'd used the correct words. "I hear that in this suburb there are killer apes." The two men set down their glasses. Without turning their heads, their eyes met. Then they looked at the bartender, who was staring at them. In unison, they all shook their heads no.

"So, it is not true," I asked in my best, yet still broken French. The man nearest to me rubbed his scruffy brown mustache. "You want to speak English here, huh?" he said still not looking at me. Which I found odd since I had switched to bad French. Then he added: "I'm not going to answer your questions. Go back to Paris."

Slightly shaken, I did just that. I briskly walked two blocks to the subway station and headed back to Paris. Disappointed that I didn't learn more about the killer, face-scraping suburban apes, I leaned back in my seat, took a deep breath and felt relieved that I hadn't been ripped apart by a French suburbanite.

David Farley is the author of the award-winning travel mem-oir/narrative history, An Irreverent Curiosity: In Search of the Church's Strangest Relic in Italy's Oddest Town, *and co-editor of* Travelers' Tales Prague and Czech Republic: True Stories. *He's a contributing writer at* AFAR *magazine and frequently writes for the* New York Times, *the* Washington Post, *and* National Geographic Traveler. *He now limits his monkey watching to zoos.*

SUZANNE LAFETRA

Going to the Dogs with My Mother

Dress for success in winter—more is more.

THE DAY BEFORE MY MOM AND I WERE TO LEAVE BALMY CALIfornia, the dogsledding trip suddenly struck me as insane.

I called the Wintergreen Lodge in northern Minnesota to double check that the super-double-extra-warm parkas I'd reserved would be ready. "And how's the weather there?"

"Oh, it's warm for January," chirped the woman on the other end of the line. "It's one."

One? One *degree*?

"Yah, I'm not even wearing a hat today," she sang in her cheerful Fargo-esque accent. "Yesterday was really cold, though," she said. "Minus fifty, doncha know."

Minus fifty? A full *one hundred degrees* colder than it was in my garage?

Last summer, it hadn't seemed like such a loony idea. My mom and I have always gotten along pretty well, save for some frosty stretches in my teens. But rarely do I break new ground—particularly frozen ground—with my sixty-four-year-old mom.

"You're lucky," my best friend said when I mentioned the possibility of the trip. Her mom had trouble just getting through a game of golf. "Our parents are getting old," she'd said, shaking her head.

My mom and I had flipped through the brochures in my sweltering California backyard. From the pages smiled apple-cheeked people petting fluffy, snowy dogs. Glistening icicles dangled from powdered sugary trees.

"This is going to be so cool, Mom" I said, fanning myself with a straw hat. "More lemonade?"

I didn't really think about the trip for a few months. I patted sandcastles with my kids, carved a grinning jack-o-lantern, and peered at columns of dark smoke when the Santa Anas sparked autumn fires nearby.

Then shopping for Christmas presents it hit me: We were going to the coldest spot in the continental U.S. in mid-January. What in god's name had we been thinking?

I flipped through a winter clothing catalog. *Sorel Caribou boots, rated to minus forty.* I ordered a pair for each of us.

After New Year's, my mom phoned me. "Ely, Minnesota is colder than Moscow today!" she was breathless with excitement. "Even Helsinki was warmer!"

I went to REI and bought super tundra-weight high-altitude mega-wimp fleece long johns. "I need the warmest gloves you have," I said to the bearded mountain guy in the green vest.

"Sure. Ski trip to Tahoe?"

"Nope. Dogsledding. Minnesota."

He stopped rummaging through the box of mittens. "Why?"

Good freaking question.

"With my mom."

He stared at me for about three seconds. "Try these." He handed me a package of Hot Hands, little chemical patches you slip into your gloves.

"I'll take the whole box."

"Nice day out there, folks," the pilot said as we taxied on the tarmac. "Six degrees with a slight breeze out of the northeast."

My mom and I glanced at each other. "Ha!" she said, zipping up her jacket. "That's nothing."

She whipped out her cell phone and called my step-dad. "We've landed!" she shouted into the phone. "There's snow everywhere! I'll call you later!"

In the tiny airport, I saw things I'd never seen in California. A moose head hung over the drinking fountain. Past the security checkpoint a stuffed grizzly bear pawed the air with his club-sized foot. Several women sported calf-length fur coats, looking quite toasty snuggled inside those dead animals. Why hadn't I thought of that?

"You the folks from California?" a chunk of woman in a fur-lined camouflage parka said in her singsong accent.

I nodded.

"Okey dokey, then. I'm Wanda." She motioned toward the taxi purring at the curb. She hoisted my mom's suit-case. I gazed around the blinding white landscape. "So, you guys ever seen snow before?"

We puttered out into the icy afternoon, the low winter sun glinting across the slick highway. We chugged past iron mines, a store called Chocolate Moose and a town called Embarrass. Flakes fuzzed the windows while Wanda passed back pictures of her grandkids. She asked if we'd ever felt an earthquake.

It was three-thirty and getting dark when we arrived at the Wintergreen Lodge. "Oh, you're the ones from California," said Dominic, one of our guides. We shook hands with our fellow mushers, all from the Midwest. All had nice warm hands. One was even wearing a t-shirt.

I poured steaming tea for my mom and me, and Dominic announced we'd start Dogsledding 101 after dinner. "But first, let's talk about fears and expectations."

"Yah, then we need to go over your clothing system," said Lynn Anne, the other guide. She was looking right at my mom and me.

I snuggled a little closer to the wood burning stove. One woman said she was afraid she wouldn't be able to handle the dogs. Another confessed her fear of falling through the ice. My mom didn't know if her cell phone would work in negative-degree weather. I was wondering what the hell a "clothing system" was. And my feet were cold.

I raised my hand. "Uh, I'm a little worried that my contacts are going to freeze to my eyeballs." I had read that such things could happen. I wanted to be ready.

Dominic gave me a stern look. "Don't get freaked out by the cold," he shook his shaggy head. "If you get it in your mind that you're going to be cold, you'll be miserable," he said. "Besides, it's only fifteen below."

We practiced saying "gee" for right turn, and "hike" for go. We gobbled hunks of Baked Alaska. Then Lynn Anne asked us to lay out all our cold weather gear. She picked through our multiple fleece jackets, the Polartec leggings, the boots with extra liners. "You guys are going to roast," she said. My mom and I beamed.

People started yawning, and made for their rooms. But we were still on west coast time and wide awake.

"Hey," my mom said, "let's see if we can see the northern lights." Her face glowed.

"You mean . . . outside?"

"Come on," she nudged me. "We'll try out our 'Clothing System.'"

"Okey dokey."

It took ten minutes to get suited up. I pulled on a pair of thermals. Insulated snow pants. Then a fleece jacket. Another fleece anorak, then the shell. Two pairs of socks and two hats. The minus forty Sorels. Glove liners and mittens. The Hot Hands. And the neck gaiter pulled up over my mouth, doncha know. I looked like I was ready to rob an igloo.

"Mmmffphrgg" my mom said, and poked an appendage toward the front door.

Outside, I squinched my eyelids so only a nanometer of pupil was showing and braced for the icy blast. I gripped the handrail and started down, like Neil Armstrong descending. *That's one small stair, one giant step for the thin-blooded, freaked-out, overly-dressed Californian.*

I stood in the deep snow and surveyed the wintery surroundings. The spruce trees were like giant green toothbrushes with a foot of icy white toothpaste squirted onto their branches. "You O.K.?"

My mom nodded.

We waded through the thigh deep powder on White Iron Lake. A half moon winked from behind a cluster of clouds, bathing everything in a fairy tale white. I thought of wolves. Of Robert Frost's poem. Of the ice, solid under our feet. My mom's breathing was heavy and I stopped.

"I forgot how quiet it gets in the snow," she whispered. I pulled down my neck gaiter and looked up. Tiny diamonds gleamed in the black bowl of the sky. Orion, the hunter. The dog star. Polaris.

We hadn't gazed at the stars together since I was a little girl, back when time stretched out in front of us like a long summer day.

"It's wonderful to be here together, honey" she said, and put her arm around me. Her breath hung warm in the icy air.

You're lucky, my friend's voice echoed in my head.

I nodded, and deep inside my ears I heard the shushing of my heart, the blood running hot and strong through my body.

My mom turned to smile at me. Well, she crinkled up her eyes so I assumed she was smiling, because I could only see a one-inch strip of her face.

And we were warm enough to stand together for a long time on that frozen lake, staring at the stars moving slowly but surely across the wintry sky.

Suzanne LaFetra is an award winning writer whose work has appeared in many newspapers and literary journals, including the San Francisco Chronicle, *the* Christian Science Monitor, Brevity, *on San Francisco's NPR affiliate radio station, and in many anthologies. She lives in Northern California with her children.*

The Spice is Right

I'll have what she's having!

Tacos before sex. Tacos after sex. Perhaps even sex with a guy named Taco. Sex in a taqueria though? This was the last way I was expecting to spend my Saturday afternoon. In fact, I was planning on spending it watching pirated movies alone in my Mexico City apartment. Then my stomach grumbled.

Down the street from my apartment was a little taqueria that served the best *alambre* in all of Mexico. The perfect combination of Oaxaca cheese, ham, peppers, and salsa made me question why I ever needed to cook for myself again. Truthfully though, it wasn't only the food I went for.

On that particular Saturday afternoon I grabbed my wallet and walked around the corner to the taqueria. I found the cook and owner sitting in two of the red plastic chairs that made up the twenty feet by twenty feet dining area. They looked bored out of their minds. A bottle of tequila sat on the table in front of them.

"*Hola, que onda?*" I asked.

"*Aqui*, waiting for you!" they responded cheerfully. The cook got up and started my *alambre* without me even having to order. Happily chopping up the veggies and meat to heat on the grill, he started talking of the joint taqueria he was going to open with me in Oregon one day.

"You and me, we're going to be rich," he said confidently. When the *alambre* was ready he handed me the plate along with a basket of corn tortillas.

I took my usual seat by the counter next to the owner. Already I felt nervous. I'll admit a part of me was intrigued about the gentle voiced twenty-five-year-old. His black moppy hair. That cheeky smile. A man who expressed a sincere love for tacos, french architecture, and japanese anime. He was unusually charming.

He grabbed the bottle of tequila and opened it.

"Thirsty?" he asked. I shrugged and let him pour me a shot. The three amigos—my future business partner, my Mexican infatuation, and myself—raised our shot glasses.

"*Salud!*" we said in unison and drank up.

We continued talking until I finished my *alambre*. Angel asked if I wanted to smoke out back. I nodded and followed him out the door. Surprise! The "back" was really his bedroom. Oh how smooth.

"You sleep in the taqueria?" I asked, peering in. It was exactly what one would imagine a guy like him sleeping in. A king sized bed tucked in the corner. Anime movie posters on the wall. Some odd eiffel tower knickknack sitting on his one chair desk. I hesitated at first to enter, but Angel gave me a reassuring "no problema" smile, and I went in.

"Saves on rent." He handed me a cigarette, lit it, and I then moved to examine his collection of films lying next to the television. Within seconds I felt his lips on the back of my neck. I shouldn't have been startled. Should I really be that surprised? I started making small talk about my love for Jack Black, pretending not to notice that a guy with whom my conversations had rarely gone beyond favorite taco toppings, was now moving his hand toward my bra strap. He stopped.

"Is this all right?" he asked kindly.

Is this all right? I wonder. In about 97.4% of situations, no, it probably wouldn't be. But I guess that particular afternoon the alambre aphrodisiac was too strong and my taqueria man too tempting. My mind screamed "Seize the moment Megan! He's hot!"

"*Si*," I tell him. Yes, *vamanos*, *andale*, let's do this hombre!

He spun around to face me and we started making out. The copy of *Nacho Libre* dropped to the floor, soon to be covered by our clothes. We wrapped ourselves around each other like a perfectly prepared tortilla. He is the cheese, I am the ham. No wait—I'm the jalapeno pepper and he's the picante salsa. Actually, it doesn't matter because by the time I managed to find a decent taco analogy to describe our sexual act, it's over. A bell is heard from up front. The sound of the chef talking to a customer brought us back to reality and we quickly grabbed our clothes and checked our hair in his bathroom mirror. Slightly less elegant than when I came into the room but convincingly tame enough to fool any suspicious customers. Was it just me or did I smell like chorizo?

I quickly walked through the kitchen, not able to look at the chef in the eye. He was no fool, he knew what happened. Our joint taco shop endeavor had officially been scrapped. "Out the door, out the door, out the door" was all I could think to myself. Jesus Christ. Jesus Cristo. I had sex with the taqueria guy. In his taqueria. Does this mean I don't have to pay for my alambre? Oh god, I just paid for my tacos with sex. I am officially a taco whore. An *alambre* slut.

"Let me walk you home please," Angel said to me. I motioned that I was good on my own and said I'll talk to him soon. Once back at the apartment, I found my roommates in the kitchen sifting through the box of take out menus. I glanced at the well worn taqueria flyer clutched in my friends left hand.

"Hey Megan. Hungry?"

I shook my head and left them alone to sift. The next hour was spent scrubbing any lingering scent of taco off my body in the bathroom.

Any effort on my part to avoid the taqueria for the next couple weeks was made in vain. Turns out a few days after our little incident the taco shop shut down for unexplained reasons. I never saw my taqueria lover again. Shame really. The *alambre* was *good*.

Megan Rice is a half-Oregonian, half-Welsh rock star. She's been incredibly lucky to have worked in various countries in Latin America and Europe and she's just getting started. Having recently gone through a quarter life crisis, she now embraces a life of words, art, love, and pure madness.

KATIE EIGEL

Drug Money

Desperately seeking a hit of culture.

"Mom, Dad, can I borrow some money for drugs?" I asked on a phone call from Switzerland to Missouri. Actually, it didn't come out like that. But that's what I meant. When you ask your parents if you can go to Amsterdam, you're basically asking for drug money.

My parents, whose nerves were already frayed from worrying what their twenty-year-old daughter really "studied" 5,000 miles away from home, were speechless. I knew better. I had asked if I could go to Holland as opposed to Amsterdam, thinking that visions of tulips, windmills, and wooden clogs swirling in my parents' minds would still secure my slot as favorite daughter.

They raised me as a trustworthy, Midwestern Catholic girl, so I meant no harm. (Oddly enough, the first time I met marijuana was on a school prayer retreat.) At the time, my worldly curiosity burned stronger than my Catholic guilt of committing venial sins.

Funny thing was, I could smoke pot in Switzerland; it was decriminalized, but that wasn't good enough. I needed bragging rights. I was a gullible American who bought into the idea that one had to venture to some top-ten-list

destination for the "Best Places to Get High." If someone bragged about smoking pot in Switzerland to other
home-bodied Americans, who have not heard of the place
via mass media, the adventure doesn't hold up. It would
have been a lot cheaper, and possibly more scenic, to get
high in a lush Swiss park surrounded by the Alps. My dad
always told me, "Go big or go home." Although that was
the last thing he would say in reference to Amsterdam
debauchery.

"Why do you want to go to Holland?" asked my Dad.

As I stood in my Swiss studio apartment staring out at
the mountaintops, I could picture Mom and Dad side-by-
side in their rocking chairs, looking out onto the peaceful, picket-fence backyard dotted with Gingko trees. If I
couldn't spin-doctor this one, they were in for small-town
shock.

"Well," I said as my voice cracked, "we met some people in Italy who are from there and we want to visit them."

Silence.

"Annnnnnd," I stretched, trying to break the awkwardness, "there's so much art and culture there, like Van Gogh.
It'd be really cool."

Still nothing from the other end, so I threw in the
phrase that any college student did when hopes for inde-
pendence grew slim.

"It's a once-in-a-lifetime chance. While I'm over here, I
should take advantage of it, right?"

"You're not going to go to Amsterdam are you?" asked
my Dad in a tone that verged on using my full name.

"Well, maybe. I mean, just for a day trip or something.
Sooo . . . can I go?"

My Mom finally caved. "We'll put some money in your
account. But don't do anything stupid." Mom was, and still
is, always right.

I hung up the phone, looked at my roommate, Jan, who sat on the bottom bunk in our bedroom, which was also our living room and dining room.

"I can go!"

"Shut up!"

"I know!"

We hugged each other and raced five feet from our multi-purpose room into our kitchen, which housed our matching laptops. I booked the flight I found prior to my phone call.

Jan and I didn't know much about Amsterdam. And for two naive Missourians, we had no business going there. Neither of us wanted to pay for art museums, let alone hardcore drugs, or fornication. We were, however, willing to pay for recreational activities that Americans can't legally do.

With little research, our city map, and the address to one coffee shop, we headed out from the main train station, which dropped us off in front of the area's main canal. Tour boats passed each other. Families crossed over bridges holding hands. Triangular-shaped buildings, all the same height, lined the canal.

We set out on foot and learned the importance of dodging bikes on the streets and sidewalks. Bicycles arched their ways across the cobblestone bridges and hugged the base of every tree and street pole.

There was something about this city that made me think it kept a big secret. A good secret. A secret it would share as soon as you showed a genuine interest. This secret we found in the ubiquitous cafes. Everyone inside appeared calm and peaceful. A few patrons sat at tables and read newspapers while slowly exhaling ghostly streams. Alternately lifting cigarettes, espresso cups, and newspapers. We wanted to be among this group, so in we went.

"How do you ask for weed?" Jan whispered to me as we walked in trying to look like we've done this before.

"I don't know. I never bought it."

"Maybe you just ask?"

We sat down, placed our jackets on the chair backs, and glanced around trying to fit in.

One young woman worked the counter.

"Vhut can I get you tourists something?" she said.

"Ah . . ." I glanced at Jan's open-mouth smile. She was the happy-go-lucky blonde who always got what she wanted. Not because she was seductive, because she was flirty.

"Umm, we want some weed." Spoken like a true sub-urbanite who was trying to score pot in a chain-restaurant parking lot.

"Virst timer?" the waitress guessed.

"Yes," Jan said with a friendly you-figured-us-out laugh. I laughed, too.

"Zen I split yous hassish bar."

She pulled out a candy bar in a brown wrapper that said, "Stoners." It resembled the font and colors of Snickers.

"Very strong. Eat little. Vait, zen more; not thing whole."

"How much?" I asked.

"Sten Euro."

Sold. Jan and I giggled when the waitress turned to get change.

"Are we really going to do this?" said Jan.

"No turning back now," I said as I tore open the Stoners.

It looked like a Snickers, too. I broke one-quarter off and slime green ooze gelled onto the wrapper. It stuck to my finger and I licked it off.

Down went piece number one. It tasted the same way pot smells, like a skunk that got thrown through a pine tree. Maybe it would slowly ease into our systems, like the first drag of nicotine jogging through the nervous system, but nothing. We were antsy to feel mellow.

"Let's go exploring," Jan said.

We strolled down a lively, narrow street. No room for cars, just people, bikes, cafes, and chintzy-gift shops. Jan and I ducked into a few shops to look for miniature clogs. Still no high, so we ate more Stoners.

Our next move brought us to a thrift shop. When I spotted an entire wall rack filled with Lacoste polos, I freaked out. All colors perfectly arranged like the rainbow. My jaw dropped, and I started laughing. Then I hugged the shirts.

"Oh my God, I'm in heaven!" I exclaimed. At the same time I thought, I'm high as hell! I tried on one of every color.

The sales lady piled up stacks outside the dressing room. I threw them on two at a time, popping up the bottom collar over the top one for a layered effect. For an hour, I modeled in the mirror.

I got higher and higher. Gaining control of myself for moments at a time, it occurred to me how high I actually was before my mind floated back to space. I couldn't stop grinning, a sign real stoners call "perma-grin." I thought I would never be normal again; this would never wear off. My brain tingled. I opened my mouth and stretched it into big circles. In that dressing room, I morphed into a kid who discovered her shadow for the first time.

"Jan," I said. "I feel liked I'm getting hugged, not physically—but psychologically. Let's get something to eat!"

"Ooo, falafels!" Jan shouted for all to hear.

When most young Americans venture out into the world for the first time, an incredible thing happens—they discover Middle Eastern cuisine. Doner kebabs. Hummus. Falafels. And hookahs. All foreign objects to me in Missouri.

"What time is it?" I asked.

Jan laughed at her watch, "Seventy eleven o'clock. So like two p.m. or something?"

Our Amsterdam adventure totaled two hours. It seemed like ten.

Tack on the extra hour it took us to order and eat the damn falafel because Jan and I couldn't control the giggles. We spent only a half hour eating it, during which we proclaimed, at the same sitting, our love and disgust for the meal. A few bites in, Jan tossed the cucumber-sauce-soaked wax paper into the trash and we went back to the main road.

The second the cafe door shut, my mood swung from perma-grin to paranoia. Terrible thoughts raced into my head as the sun set.

"Where are we?"

"Why is that man staring at us? Has he been following us?"

"What if someone breaks into our room and steals our stuff?"

Wait a minute. What room? As we carried our oversized backpacks with us, it dawned on me that we hadn't booked a hostel.

I grabbed Jan and flung us into the nearest hotel. Cost wasn't an issue. Mom and Dad could worry about that bill. I remained too paranoid about people stealing my polo shirts. Once we booked lodging, Jan left me inside to get more munchies. She discovered chocolate Hit cookies. I discovered Euro MTV.

We ate every cookie and passed out. We woke up in the exact clothes from the previous day with MTV still blaring. I rolled over onto cookie crumbs and crumpled receipts to check the clock. My hair smelled like an ashtray. My ponytail wrestled its way to the right side of my head. My mascara smeared to my cheekbones.

I had a hangover like no other—one nauseated by guilt. The whole "oops-I-ate-a-hash-bar-and-got-stoned-off-my-ass-for-hours story" was not the respectable proof of money well spent that I needed.

Jan rolled over, "What time is it?

"It's time to get up. We're going to an art museum," I said.

Katie Eigel is a digital marketing professional—whatever that means. Originally from Missouri, she has lived in Chicago, Switzerland, San Francisco, Arizona, and currently New York city. When not city hopping, she enjoys splurging on wine and traveling on the cheap. You can follow her adventures on Twitter @eieigel.

Karma at the Colombo Airport

*It's best to keep your karma within reach—
in your carry-on bag.*

IT WAS ALL TOO CLEAR, WHEN I CAME DOWN WITH A VIOLENT, upwardly mobile stomach bug on my last day in South Asia, that I had accrued some seriously bad karma.

My episode of feet-slapping, stomach-buckling sprints to the bathroom, cloaked in the midnight steam room heat of our Colombo apartment, began just hours before our flight back to Los Angeles, after seven weeks in Sri Lanka—on the one day we didn't eat street food but splurged on a beachfront fancy restaurant with a Frenchy name. The chances that this food on this day would make me sick were too absurd.

Besides, we were in a country of tens of thousands of Buddha statues, in which saffron-clad monks are the highest-class rank, and everything happens for a reason.

Halfway through the trip, my partner, Aruna, who is Sri Lankan by blood and literally begins to glow after a few weeks in the heat and humidity, got laid up for three days in our Colombo apartment with his own nasty, delirium-inducing

stomach bacteria. After he recovered, I trilled on about having a stomach of steel and being safe from all manner of
invasive critters because I was a vegetarian.

A few weeks after that, Aruna and I lied, saying I was
sick, to get out of one of many compulsory audiences with
a group of extremely extended family members. When
they showed up at our door in Kandy anyway, offering
stackable stainless steel containers of rice and curry, we
were caught, red-faced and ashamed, and I found myself
putting on a good show of having a fit of loose bowels.

So really, it made a lot of sense that I would be hit with
a day of "nonstop vomiting," as Aruna's mother knowingly
called it, just in time for our thirty-hour journey home.

When it got to the point that I couldn't stand up
straight and couldn't even keep down the lime and garlic
tincture a local friend made for me, we knew we couldn't
just wait it out. But it was 3 A.M., the Ayurvedic clinic
next door didn't have an emergency division, and there
were no hospitals listed in the Lonely Planet. Luckily, the
taxi we had reserved to take us to the airport was able to
come early and knew of a private clinic. Ten dollars and a
couple suppositories later—prescribed by a steely woman
doctor who asked me only my first name, my age, and my
symptoms, and administered by a nurse who looked to
be about fourteen-years old—we were on our way to the
Bandaranaike International Airport.

The good news was, thanks to a tactic I had devised of
hanging half-mast, Uttanasana-style and quietly moaning,
I made it through two hours of waiting in line for check-
in and customs without puking on anyone. Well, almost.

Just as our customs official was scrutinizing our pass-
ports, carefully stamping and initialing this and that, it
became clear I could last no longer.

Even though I'm pretty sure this a high-ranking sign
you're a terrorist, I dropped my carry-on, grabbed my

passport from the official's hands and galloped, convulsively bucking, toward the terminal. Aruna stammered apologies behind me as I begged an unsympathetic luggage clerk, "Bathroom?!" without breaking my gait.

It's amazing how quickly the mind works when you're about to vomit. I imagine this lucidity is akin to "life flashing before your eyes" as you await death, or "going internal" just as you're about to give birth.

Something inside me calculated the exact seconds I had until eruption, and, like the Terminator's computerboard mind identifying John Connors, I zeroed in on a nearby standing ashtray as my target.

The whole mess couldn't have been better choreographed by Danny Boyle. Just as bile was coursing up my gullet, I flung myself, long-jumper style, across the final stretch, shoving an unassuming woman in a sari out of my path, and retched a thin mixture of water and dehydration salts into the narrow receptacle.

As I whimpered, spat and snotted into the ashtray, Aruna patting my back, handing me tissues, and apologizing to the woman I'd taken down, I thought, trembling:

You win this one, Buddha. You win this one.

★

Jessica Langlois has an MFA in Creative Nonfiction and works as a freelance journalist and instructor in English composition. Her writing has appeared in American Literary Review, *the* East Bay Express, *and the* Oakland Tribune, *and she is the creative nonfiction editor for* Generations Literary Journal. *She is currently at work on a memoir about her mother's life in Austria, and her and her sister's relationships to their mysterious paternity. She blogs about travel, pop culture, and nostalgia at www.asupposedlyfunthing.com.*

Hollywood Fiction

A writer discovers what he really wants is to direct!

IT'S A HALF-HOUR TO MIDNIGHT ON NEW YEAR'S EVE AND I'm standing in the private bathroom of a Hollywood night club. I tower over the well-styled mane of one of Tinsel Town's D-list actors—whose name escapes me, because he's a friend, of a friend, of someone I just met. He tries to induce vomiting. He gets some on my shoe and I just ignore it, as I've uncomfortably assumed a role as his narcotics man-servant. How I got into this club, with these people, to this moment, is some part due to indifference, boredom and chaotic fluke. It also seems to be the envy of every mediocre, next-big-thing.

But all I want is for this evening to end.

The D-list actor turns his head up from the toilet bowl and says, "Pass me the bag." Bag? What bag? I think, ". . . *over there*," he motions to the hand basin.

"Oh sorry," I say, wondering why I'm apologizing? Maybe it's because I'm unconsciously contributing to his early death, ". . . here you go."

"Nice huh," he says referring to the ornate man-bag, "I got it custom made by this guy on Sunset . . . they also do one for H."

"Really? I'm more of a pot man myself." He doesn't get my sarcasm.

I then hear the sound of a gag and see his mop-top flip over. He's passing out on the toilet floor, his disoriented eyes, looking up to the marble ceiling. He's almost motionless—and I have my hands full of his accoutrements.

"I'm O.K. This shit happens to me sometimes."

This is my cue to exit—stage left, or right—the hell out of this Hollywood drama.

It's a slight deviation to my Los Angeles package holiday. I could be at the pre-arranged New Year's Eve celebration near the Staples Center; enjoying a nice glass of champagne with fat middle-aged tourists and recounting the sightseeing adventures of the last few days.

They were having lobster.

It's funny the places you can get into in Los Angeles with a foreign accent and a velvet Armani blazer. Never mind the Target jeans. If you think you belong—then people don't assume otherwise. This half-cocked strategy, that was a departure from my norm, seemed to be working tonight.

Still, what was hard to reconcile, was going from eating baby back ribs on Santa Monica Pier that afternoon, to talking about rhinoplasty with two gorgeous actresses, earlier that night. They both had come from the Midwest to make it big in Hollywood.

"So what do you do in England?" gorgeous actress number one asked me.

"I'm from Australia, actually," I yelled over the music. She didn't hear me but she nodded anyway. "I'm an urban planner."

"You're a painter?" asked gorgeous actress number two.

"Painting—yeah I'm an artist," I said without compunction, realizing that I wouldn't see these people ever again. But there's also something intoxicating about Hollywood that makes you want to exaggerate with others—to be a cooler, manufactured version of yourself.

"Oh, I love artists," said gorgeous actress number one. I started to get it: the universal appeal to twenty-somethings of appearing to be a Bohemian fly-by-the-seat-of-the-pants illusion always trumps the secure, respected, corporate clone. These thoughts helped me to justify my own Hollywood fiction for the rest of the night.

"Yeah, I do a lot of modern abstract art, but it's writing that I love," I said, realizing I know nothing about art.

"You're a writer too," one of them said—not sure who, as both they started looking the same. "Do we know any of your work?"

Normally, I can't stand those liars, who build false expectations, lead you into emotional nirvana and then, strip it all away in an instant, but it was different in Hollywood. Everyone seemed to bullshit each other out here and maybe they needed to do this, to make life more palatable.

"Maybe—done a bit here and there." I unsuccessfully tried to think of some magazines that they wouldn't know. "Um, I've done a piece for *Rolling Stone* . . . others for *GQ*, um . . . and *Harper's Bazaar*," I said, then realizing that I'd never read *Harper's Bazaar*.

"Wow," said the same gorgeous actress, "You're like a real writer. Can we Google some of your work?"

I was in deep shit.

"Yeah it should be on there, but um . . . um, it's the Australian syndicated version of *Rolling Stone* you see—they just don't make it available on the net."

"Oh that's too bad."

"Never mind. I can send you a hard copy by post when I get back to Sydney if you like. How about I get your number?" I said with a cheeky smile.

With a speed akin to Clint Eastwood in some cowboy movie, they drew out business cards. In the dim light of the club I could make out glamour head-shots, the word "actress" in cursive script, contact details, and on the back—bullet-points outlining the bit parts they'd played on stage and screen.

Two hours later, I found myself speaking to four more would-be movie stars—three guys and a girl—on an eco-friendly pleather couch. They were all friends of the two gorgeous actresses.

"So are you working on anything at the moment for *Rolling Stone* or *GQ*?" asked Josh, a multi-media artist that works on Hollywood movies.

Not this again. I started to re-think my lies.

"Yeah I have a few ideas for a story but nothing developed yet—maybe something about Australian bands trying to make it in the LA music scene," I said, trying to divert the focus to an area, I hoped, they knew little about.

"Oh that's cool, I love Australian music. Wolfmother's latest album is just so progressive—I have it on my iPod. Who do you think is going to be big this year?" then asked Eric, a twenty-three-year-old theatre arts graduate from NYU, now living in Culver City.

I made a mental note to self: Google "Wolfmother" when back at the hotel.

"Well they are progressive . . . but you know," I said again, trying to cover-up, "I like LA music like the Red Hot Chilli Peppers—aren't they from around here?"

"Yeah—they met in Hollywood High," said Chris, another twenty-something too-cool-for-school non-actor, wearing a fur-lined parka and mirrored sunglasses (inside the club).

It was then the conversation went from local bands to auditions; workouts and diets for auditions; drugs for auditions and finally to sex—for auditions. I was amongst the blasé and almost mechanical discussion of making it in Hollywood. Everyone knew what was expected, and the price that needed to be paid, if you weren't an exceptional actor.

Chris's girlfriend, the beautiful brunette, Stacey—who was thinking of becoming a blonde, and getting her stage name legalized, told me that she didn't go to college. Instead, she studied a three-month acting course with a well-known acting coach in LA. She seemed confident of her skills, as she assumed the pose of a celebrity being interviewed and said, "All I need is to get that break on like a sitcom or even a speaking part on a hit summer movie—and then I'll be famous!" She laughed at this, and meant it to be tongue-in-cheek, but the rest of the group nodded in solemn agreement. I realized then, that they were not interested in developing the craft of acting, but in the fame game, and this was O.K. for them. But this was a Hollywood nightclub on New Year's Eve, when illusion and artifice were in good supply—including my own.

Amid all my amateur and unintended fiction, I did make one slip-up that night. I asked Eric, the more intelligent one of the group, "What happens if it doesn't work out for you as an actor in LA?"

He looked at me in disgust, covered partly by the low-light of the nightclub and said in a cool, calculated voice, "Don't ever ask me that. The truth is, you can't think that way—I'm going to be here until I make it big—no other options for me." If he hadn't said it with such conviction, I would have offered him some sort of faux-brotherly advice, that he should do something else more fulfilling with his life. He was smart enough; law school, med school or even barber school—anything was more certain than a life chasing a one-in-a-million dream, based on looks—assuming he wasn't an exceptional actor.

Some minutes later, the two gorgeous actresses, Josh, Eric, Chris and Stacey; as well as one of their acquaintances—and whom I only remember as the D-list actor, with a mop-top, all adjourned into a private bathroom. The D-list actor produced an ornate and somewhat gaudy man-bag.

A few more minutes later, I watched them all slowly enter a better dream, than the one they all shared.

I leave LA at eleven the next morning with the middle-aged tour group. They all seem to have had a good time in the restaurant near the Staples Center. They tell me how I missed out on the lobster, and how the German couple kept dancing all night, even when there was no music.

"Where did *you* go last night?" asks one of the Dutch guys. "We had lobster . . . and lots of single elderly ladies on the dance floor—missed your chance." He nudges his wife.

"Probably not my thing really—more a Dutch thing I reckon." His wife is incensed. I remember why I didn't go with the group.

I sit watching LA slip into the distance, as the tour group starts singing show tunes on the way to Las Vegas. In my mind, I'm reliving last night. No holiday tour or Universal Studios ride could have shown me that side of Hollywood. I think of my own fiction last night, and how it enabled me to witness the LA kind: the artifice of keeping one's dreams alive.

As we enter Nevada and see the bright lights of Las Vegas in the desert dusk. I realize that I'm going into another land of fiction—a land of wedding chapels and $4.99 buffets. Only this time it's back to the real me.

And the lobster is included.

★

Troy Rodrigues is an Australian writer and photographer who has since traded his briefcase for a backpack and set forth in search of more tales of mayhem. He officially calls Sydney home, though Paris will always be a lofty aspiration.

ALLISON J. STEIN

Naked, with a Passport

Staring would be the polite thing to do.

"Madam, is it fine?"

I opened my eyes with some effort, as my entire face, including my eyelashes, were coated in sesame oil.

The young woman was pointing at my ear. She was apparently asking me whether it was okay to massage it.

Well, let's see. I was in Kerala, India. I'd already stripped naked with this very woman standing not more than three inches from my elbow. I had allowed her to seat me on a chair in the middle of the room, brightly lit by unflattering flourescent lights. She proceeded to pour the aforementioned sesame oil all over my head—the beginnings of a traditional Ayurvedic massage. As she led me to the wooden massage table, I noticed the door was more than slightly ajar; as spa staff and other clients walked past, they peered into the room. I closed my eyes. She got started on the massage proper, which was a very good one. At some point, another woman walked in to the room and joined her—a personnel addition I hadn't been expecting—and with businesslike head-to-toe strokes, together they left no part of me untouched.

So after all of that, I wasn't about to fuss over the sanctity of my ear.

"Sure," I croaked. I was hoping my tone would be casual, easygoing. I cleared my throat, tried again. "Why not," I squeaked.

She put her fingers shallowly into my ear canal and pulled them out with a small pop. And then she gestured for me to get up, and wrapped her arms around my waist once I was standing, to keep me from falling since my feet were slick. We minced down the hallway towards the shower, I wearing nothing but my oily shine. We passed about a dozen or so women in the hallway—clients also naked, staff in saris. Everyone smiled at me.

I have no idea what expression I had on my face. Because here's the thing: I'm not someone who is really comfortable with public or even semi-public nudity. I'm not a nudist and have never been to a nude beach, haven't once considered mooning or streaking. I was not a Girl Gone Wild in college, I don't even wear very short shorts or extremely low-cut shirts. Slithering around an Ayurvedic center naked in the company of many others did not exactly put me in my happy place. And yet, no one was forcing me to do it. I could have bailed out; and what's more I certainly would have if I'd been there with anyone I knew, a friend, or—horrors—a colleague.

But the fact of the matter is, if I'm traveling solo and you ask me to strip in the name of an interesting spa experience, say, a Turkish hammam, a Japanese bath, I'll start to unzip and unbutton. I'll confess to feeling pride about this tendency of mine. I've always considered my willingness to peel off my skivvies at appropriate moments as a my "real traveler" badge of honor, with extra points awarded since it makes me uncomfortable *and* since it's not something that I would be willing to do at home.

Which is pretty weird if you think about it. I mean, why should it feel safer to be naked and vulnerable in front of foreign strangers than among friends and familiarity? And yet, it seems a common weirdness. There's a whole range of semi-public-to-public naked activities that typically occur while traveling that aren't in the category of sex tourism—spas, clothing-optional beaches, wet t-shirt contests. Many women do seem more willing to expose more of themselves abroad than they do at home. Does travel make it easier for a woman to overcome "the curse of Eve," i.e., modesty?

It sure seemed like it was for me.

That is, until I visited Baden Baden, Germany. I'd gone to take the waters, as they say, in this historic spa town, and had my pick of the town's brand new facility, which looked like a YMCA in a really nice neighborhood, or the Friedrichsbad, which is the 133-year-old Irish-Roman bath. Of the half million people who visit the bathing complex each year, only 70,000 visit the older facility, and among these are very, very few Americans. That's because the Friedrichsbad is nudist: no bathing suits allowed.

Guess which one I picked? It was only after I was handed the wrist-band gizmo to operate my locker that I learned one more piece of critical info: several days a week, the Friedrichsbad is co-ed. And this was one of those days.

Oh.

This was indeed a novelty—all my previous experiences with nudity while traveling have been strictly girls-only. I haven't been naked in the company of groups that included strange men since the day I was born. Also I'm a married lady. A spa typically poses no challenge to my most important commitment, whereas this situation suggested the possibility of something a bit more outré. I stood in the locker room, hesitating. Could this small town on the edge of the Black Forest, with all its well-manicured gardens, possibly be concealing a bawdy swingers scene . . . right in this historic landmark? I stood very still and listened. I didn't hear the telltale *buh-buh-baum-chick* of porno music. I continued unzipping and unbuttoning and made myself a deal: I'd keep my eyes on the exit and if I heard or saw anything creepy I'd get right out. I went in.

The Friedrichsbad consists of seventeen different stations of saunas, steams and soaks of different temperatures. You are obliged to move through these stations in order. On the wall, maps indicated the direct path, which siphoned you towards the center of the building—a grand, domed rotunda, supported by arches and columns that rise from marble floors. It's like a museum with the nude sculptures come to life.

I didn't see many people at the first few stations— this was the middle of a weekday afternoon—but under the rotunda there were about a dozen people, men and women, in the soaking pools. I kept a sharp eye out, but everyone seemed with absolutely no effort to keep their gaze about six inches in front of their toes while walking, and at a fuzzy middle distance when nonchalantly soaking. In fact, when I looked around to see if anyone was looking at any one else, I was the only one with a wandering gaze.

This observation, combined with the warm water and the steam had a soothing effect. My eyelids hovered to half open, and a feeling came over me that I recognized: I was relaxed. I felt a little silly about my internal hysterics in the locker room. *You see*, I lectured myself, *there's no reason to get so worked up about these things.* After a while, I got out of the pool and dripped my way over to the map on the wall to see where I was supposed to go next.

Okay, as a travel writer, even one who is at this very moment practically inviting you to picture her naked, I feel shy about revealing that I had trouble reading the map. I mean, the place is really old, an antique, and it was really hot, and I probably need to be adorned in a certain amount of fabric for my brain to work properly . . . anyway, I misread the damned map. So it was quite by accident that I learned another critical piece of information: only certain areas of the Friedrichsbad are co-ed.

Which I found out only after I wandered into a male-only area completely naked.

The moment I stepped into the room, I realized that all wasn't as it should be. I saw wet blonde hair and damp skin, but mostly what I registered were many many many eyes, all staring at me. And then I noticed that their mouths were moving—they were shouting, in German, at me. I understood nothing. I felt rooted to the spot. As I believe all present could confirm, my blush was very widespread.

I commanded my trembling legs to get me the hell out of there. After what seemed like a very long while, but was probably only seconds, they obeyed.

At that moment, all of my pride at being more comfortable with nudity while traveling, any sense that I had of it being a badge of travel honor, evaporated like so much steam. Although I removed all of my clothing in the locker room at the Friedrichsbad, up until the moment I stepped into the male-only area, I was not naked. Yes, I was wearing nothing, but I was also appropriately dressed for the occasion. I was also wearing a suitable outfit in the Ayurvedic spa. There's nothing particularly brave about blending in, especially when you consider that I only would do it when I was traveling solo—without a friend or a colleague or some other emissary of home, an anchor to my familiar definition of nudity.

So ask me again whether travel can be a cure for a woman's modesty, and I'll say yes—but only on a definitional technicality. I'll take advantage of that technicality in my future travels, but now that I know that I'm only situationally immodest, I'll proceed with the utmost caution. Of this I'm certain: there's a nudity taboo out there that I could haplessly violate; somewhere, a variety of Eve's apple lurks. And I'd really rather not take another bite.

Allison J. Stein is an award-wining writer and essayist. She's the culinary travel guide for About.com, and writes for Perceptive Travel. *She's contributed to* Business Week, Glamour, Men's Journal, New York Magazine, World Hum, Yankee *and* Yoga Journal *among other publications. She lives in New York's Hudson Valley.*

The Nakuru Scam

Beware of men bearing lug nuts.

"Right. Left. Right and right again. Straight on." One of the Kenyans shouted directions.

The jeep was careering through a maze of alleyways.

"Right." We lurched round a bend into a rutted lane, barely the width of the vehicle. A high, barred gate loomed ahead and the jeep screeched to a halt. One of the two Kenyans riding outside, leapt down and opened it. My husband drove through and the African closed the gate behind with a sickening thud. Within minutes the three Kenyans had removed the front wheels of the jeep and we were stranded, our vehicle immobilized, in an African township.

It had seemed a good idea at the time: to hire a jeep in Nairobi and then drive up country to Nakuru National Park to see the flamingos. The jeep was a bit dodgy. No oil registered on the dipstick. There was no water in any of the battery cells but nothing major went wrong until we reached the dusty outskirts of the town of Nakuru. As my husband negotiated a narrow rutted road seething with traffic, he suddenly noticed that there was too much play in the steering. The market stalls piled high with fruit and vegetables by the side of the road, only added to his difficulties. So did the pedestrians weaving in and out of the rusting lorries and jam-packed buses and the mangy dogs nosing rotting refuse in the gutters. Suddenly three Africans ran out in front of the jeep.

My husband slowed and before we could do anything to stop them, the men had clambered aboard.

"The ball joints on your track rod ends have gone," shouted the only one that could speak English. "But we can get it fixed."

Dazed, confused, disorientated, my husband turned the jeep. Once we had left the main road, we found ourselves in a maze of twisting alleyways.

"Right! Left. Right and right again. Straight on."

The lanes and alleys became narrower and narrower, until the final passage in this interminable labyrinth was barely the width of the jeep. Through a blur of shimmering heat, I was vaguely aware of tin roofed huts, tall black fences, piles of rusting machinery and rolls of barbed wire. Suddenly we were facing a high, barred gate. One of the men leapt out of the jeep and opened it. My husband drove through. The gate was slammed and locked behind us.

Once behind closed gates inside the compound, Joe, the English speaking Kenyan explained that he would need to go to a maintenance depot to buy the spare parts that were required to repair our vehicle.

"You will have to come with me, to pay," he explained to my husband, who nodded and before I could say, 'What about me?' The pair had disappeared.

I was left with the two non-English speaking "mechanics" who both lay down under the jeep and promptly went to sleep. As I tried to huddle into the shade of one of the tinned roofed buildings that surrounded the compound, first one then two, then more and more children began to filter out from doorways and passages. The youngest, barely three, snotty nosed and wearing only a grubby white tee shirt was clutching the hand of a gangling youth of about fifteen. All the children were bare foot, the boys dressed in frayed shorts, the girls in brightly colored shifts. White teeth gleaming in shining black faces they appeared indifferent to the heat, which lay, a thick blanket on the unmoving air.

The oldest boy spoke: "What do you do mama?"

"Teach," I said nervously. The smile on the boy's face faded.

"Music," I offered.

"Sing a song," he ordered, the smile restored.

I'm a music teacher by trade and used to performing to children so I sang, "Sun Arise," the Aborigine song that Rolf Harris popularized. It went down well. I followed with: "When you're happy and you know it clap your hands." The children applauded wildly and joined in the actions. Dizzy with success, I was just launching into "I'm a little teapot" (I taught infants for a bit), when my husband and Joe returned with the spare parts.

My husband looked at me like they do, so I stopped singing and told the children that it was their turn now. They needed no second asking. There was a swift consultation. Within seconds all the children were singing and in three-part harmony. Then they began to dance. The mechanics woke up and joined in as did various women who had drifted out of the adjoining houses. I was enchanted and very impressed. Music it seems crosses all boundaries. Still singing, the mechanics accomplished the repair and then they reinstalled the wheels. The "repair" was accomplished, the wheels set back in place and the gates reopened. Joe agreed to guide us back onto the road that led to the National Park.

It was time to say "Goodbye" to the children. The oldest boy shook my hand. I wanted to give him a present and searched my bag frantically but found only a biro.

"Sorry. That's all I have."

"It is enough,' he said with great dignity."

We saw the flamingos. They were magnificent but an anticlimax after the children. Anyway, still unsure whether we had been conned or not we set off back to our hotel. On the road that lead out of road we had the answer. Three Africans leapt out from the side of the road. They pointed to the front of the car. One shouted,

"Your track rods are broke."

We drove on.

Slyvie Downes's articles have been published in the travel magazines Italy, Times Educational Supplement, Music Education, *and* Mslexia. *Her short stories and an anthology of poetry* Signals in the Dark, *and a comic novel* Changing Places *have also been published.*

JENNIFER MASSONI

Embedded in the Boot

A traveler finds herself hobbled by circumstance.

The sliding glass doors at the Italian First Aid Room welcome and release the local Livornese with respective emergencies, most comparable to mine. The more severe cases are expedited through the waiting room to the back of the hospital, which is cut off by another set of rubber-rimmed doors I am waiting to walk through for an x-ray. Or hobble through, rather. A tenderness in my left foot has throbbed from an annoying hint back home in San Francisco to a sharp, localized spike of pain upon arrival in phonetically delightful Castiglioncello (rhymes with *limoncello*).

This Tuscan seaside town is also where my mother and I have rented a little apartment thirty yards from the edge of the Tyrrhenian Sea so she may immerse herself in language lessons and I may attempt sculpture and watercolor classes (even though any artistic "talent" last surfaced in time for the third grade art fair). But what if a visit to the Provence of our ancestors will entice its return? We are also taking a respite from my mother's second divorce and my impulsive departure from a pre-pre-revenue Internet company that was—I'll go with "mismanaged." What else would an Italian mother-daughter duo do, but cash in their frequent flyer miles and answer an ad for a two-week Tuscan escape from it all?

But now I fear I have a stress fracture from training for a half-marathon, which I registered for in a fit of self-discipline. The suspicious metatarsal is warm to the touch, swelling before my eyes, and I can't successfully stand on tiptoe. We are at the hospital in the first place thanks to the generosity of my mother's soon-to-be Italian instructor, Valentina. She sports a pair of leather, fur-lined high-tops, and she tells me where to find them in town. That is, if we ever get out of here and if I can ever again place my foot on the ground without wincing. For now we cram into hard plastic seats, the concave shape of which stopped being comfortable on hour number three; we're now approaching seven. *Si, sette ore,* which I can pronounce thanks to Valentina's impromptu day-long language lesson. I also memorize *io sono paziente*: I am patient.

While I'm being patient, my mind zooms to what will surely become a trip spent with a foot casted in a plastic boot in the very country famous for its uncanny resemblance to, of all things, a boot. When I am finally wheeled in for the x-ray, my foot is positioned on the cold table and zapped with a quick buzz of radiation in all of ten seconds. Much to my relief, my foot is *non fratturato*, and my boot-shaped fantasies dissipate. However, this marks the end of the diagnosis. I keep the x-ray for my first Italian souvenir, pay my 20-euro fee, and leave with instructions to ice and elevate.

Two days later, my mother and I greet the day from our balcony and its decadent views of the blue-gray sea that crowns Castiglioncello's scattered treetops. Despite the beauty surrounding us, I miss running. Daily exertion clears my brain of its anxious loops and an elevated heart rate acts as a full-body cleanser.

"Well, the sea is right there," my mother says.

Perfect! I will become an open-water swimmer! Right after I revive my inner artist.

My Austrian art teacher, Christian, is a sculptor and painter of some European renown. For my first lesson, I cross the gravel driveway outside the apartment, walk through the small grove of olive trees, and emerge. The sea is vast and audible, capable of astonishing the air right out of my lungs. The promenade weaves into view on the right, and I can eye the path my mother walks to her school. But my lessons are right here at the rim of the country where my great-grandparents were born, and I feel I've won a lottery I didn't know I had entered.

My fellow art students set up their easels. One is already reproducing the central tower of Castello Pasquini, the sixteenth century castle for which the town is named. In fact, Castiglioncello boasts an impressive artistic history, from cinema's Marcello Mastroianni, who won acting honors the world over to nineteenth century art's Giovanni Fattori, who made famous the landscapes I look upon now.

Oh, and there's me. Christian has me do a "quick, little sketch" to assess my "talent," but after a rather phallic rendition of the castle's tower, it is obvious that painting may not be my forte while in Italy. So Christian hands me ten pounds of soapstone and a narrow metal chisel.

"What do you want to sculpt? To see emerge from this rock?!" His eyes flare and recede with the efficient swish of a cape.

I stare at the lopsided stone. "A ball?"

Christian pouts. "Is that really all you see?"

He has a point. I take a closer look and slide the chisel against the stone, producing a soft "soapy" powder light enough to lift into the air, onto clothes, perhaps even out to sea. After a careful pause, I notice the slope of a curving backbone. "An elephant!" I shout.

Smiling with pride, Christian helps me position the chisel and hits the top handle with a quick knock of a hammer. Sure enough, a clean shard falls away, and so begins my attempt to free *un elefante* from flaking chips of stone.

After class, my new exercise regime awaits. My mother and I take the shallow steps down to the promenade. Most of the seaside bodegas have already closed their painted shutters for the season and no longer bustle with vacationing *famiglie*, their laughter and summer cavorting mere memories that lilt on offshore breezes. We veer left at a pace set by my hobbling until we find a stretch of sand and an open *gelateria*.

Even though the Tyrrhenian Sea isn't frigid to the touch like the Northern California Pacific I'm used to, no one else is in the water, save a lone snorkeler and a collection of wet-suited surfers paddling past the low stone jetty to the break between the harbor and a dark scattering of rocks. But I'm intimidated to frolic in my bikini so close to the idle men on the shore: the older set wearing various shades of beige are harmless enough, but the much younger and shirtless *uomini* have lingering eyes and flirt with occasional hollers.

Instead, I carry out a far better plan. I walk down the *other* side of the jetty, the one with a convenient concrete walkway meant for accommodating boats. I step gingerly into the lapping water, occasionally glancing back at my mother, as if I'm five (instead of twenty-eight) and learning to swim. I do frolic a little as she snaps a photo and let her have this moment without the embarrassed annoyance I might exhibit Stateside. With one last step, I push off into the cooling water. Then slice. Or was that a crunch? I must have stepped on an innocuous little seashell.

"I stepped on a seashell!" I yell, both of us still smiling and oblivious. I float on my back like an otter and lift the ball of my foot into sight, as if it is now the shell I intend to crack. Instead, half a dozen black sea urchin spines sprout at electrified angles. At least two-dozen more have sunk beneath the skin, thinly exposed like worn stubs of pencil lead. My heart rate elevates, but not in the way I've missed. Did I mention it's the same foot as the running injury? This must be why there are stalls with colorful rubber booties next to the *gelateria* and outside most of the shops on the main road. Just in case you want to saunter into the sea along a barnacle-infested concrete ramp.

I cry. I've been acting five anyway so what's the harm? On my good leg, I hop to shore and rest on the jetty, not caring that I now attract attention from both sides. My mother's face twists with worry and we both take a closer look. Out of the water, the urchin incisions are no longer soothed by a salty sea bath and I can't help the sob (or six) that escape. When I muster the courage to pull on one protruding spine, blood streams then dilutes to pink along my wet skin, just like the watercolors my fellow students mixed earlier that afternoon. The strongest awareness I have is that these are foreign entities, and I want them out of my body.

One of the older men approaches. He is a short, rotund figure with a few stains on the shirt that stretches over his belly to meet his pants. (Yes, they're *beige*, at least one word that looks identical in English and Italian.) He smoothes his graying comb-over and gestures in time with inquiries that bubble melodically from his jet-black mustache. All I can make out is his name, Alfonse. My mother offers her present-tense bursts of the language, but my foot tells as straightforward a story as any. With an expression that says he's seen this all before, he whips out his wallet and pulls back greased and creased leather folds until he plucks a dull sewing needle. He floats it like a symphony conductor's baton toward my foot, which I pull back like a babe in need of protection.

Alfonse shrugs, returning the needle to its trusty home, and gestures to a small orange Fiat parked on a sloping road leading down to the promenade. We gather he can give us a ride home so we can figure our way to the hospital twenty minutes away (yes, the same *ospedale*). I can't say I would advise two women travelers to accept such an offer, even if the man in question does bear a reassuring resemblance to Danny DeVito. Still, we trust. I manage to fold myself into the compact backseat, littered with remnants of a long vehicle ownership, but where I can at least extend my pronged foot out the open window.

For anyone keeping score: Number of days in Italy: three. Trips to the hospital: two.

After Valentina once again gives us a ride, the brunette nurse behind the check-in desk nods her head with bemused recognition. The wait is only four hours this time before I see a doctor who employs a now familiar, though sterile, approach, and uses a needle to fish out the stubborn, embedded spines. He explains that they are brittle and break like glass, making excision difficult. He manages to free three or four, but I will have to be patient for the rest to surface. (I know this one, *io sono paziente.*) They can give me a tetanus shot, as the sea urchin is the bacterial equivalent of an exposed nail (or thirty), but the doctor explains that the blood-screening regulations are not the same in Italy as they are in the States. I pass on the vaccine and am sent home with tweezers and an ointment closely related to rubber cement but which should draw the spines out overnight.

In the morning, I awake eager to pull back the gauze and find all the critters defeated and dislodged. Instead, the tweezers can't even get at one solitary spindle. The next plan of attack is to soak the foot in order to loosen the skin around spines. So that means ice for the first injury, heat for the second. Without a bathtub, the *bidet* proves the most logical receptacle for soaking. I spend an hour sitting on the windowsill, my foot dangling in a disinfectant *bidet* bath as I flip through magazines. As the *bidet* drains, I hobble to the living room to twist my foot until the spines are in view, hopeful they are lined up and ready to tweeze. I push two to the surface and the release is as satisfying as any. Then it's onto the balcony with an ice pack to attend to the initial injury, a proce-dure I supplement with table wine intake, although more generally acceptable over a long lunch at the corner cafe. (I've quickly developed an appetite for *frutti di mare* and its lurking shell life.)

The next day, I limp alongside my art class to our late morning cappuccino break that arrives all of one hour into the lesson, and regale my German, Swiss, and Cana-dian classmates with my aquatic adventure.

"I've only gotten a couple out so far," I say of the sus-pects, which have turned out to be half a centimeter or so in length, little sharp nothings capable of halting physical exertion.

Christian tilts his head to the side, where his short black ponytail collapses like a paintbrush against his shoulder, and says, "One prick per day."

I take a deep breath and nod with recognition. The wisdom is succinct and as good as any advice for life, for learning a language, for getting over the physical or emo-tional injuries we bear at home and try to release far away from it all. I should know how to pace myself by now, without burning out at work, at exercise, or any of the agendas I try to overpower back home. Some pricks to the foot are a good reminder; I will force no more, but be content with no less.

"You may not get them all out. The foot is tough," he says, slapping his palm. "Some may stay down, but they should not bother you by then."

In the moment, I accept what may be beyond measured control. We walk back along the road, still drying from an early morning rain, through the grove, and to our workstations at the edge of Italy. I pick up my chisel and continue to shape the *elefante* beginning to emerge, little by little, each day. So what if a few of the tiny foreign bodies stick around? Like any worthwhile trip—and tetanus withstanding—they, too, will just have to become a part of me.

Jennifer Massoni was the Senior Editor of the Gentry family of magazines for many years. Her journalism has also appeared in Vanity Fair, Crawdaddy!, CAFÉ, California Home & Design, *and* I Love Chile News. *In addition to sculpting elephants in Italy, she has written about finding ghosts in New Mexico, surfing waves in California, and making wine in Chile. In 2011, she earned her MFA in Prose from Mills College, where she won the Amanda Davis MFA Thesis in Fiction Award and the Ardella Mills Prize for Literary Composition. Ready to put her wanderlust to the test, she and her husband moved six thousand miles away to Santiago. You can follow her expat adventures and adjustments at notesfromthesouthernhemisphere .blogspot.com.*

Advice for Closet Cougars

OMG! Like, totally!

A FEW SUMMERS AGO, I SIGNED UP TO SPEND A WHOLE MONTH in Paris at a writing workshop. "Those things are for kids," my mother had said. "Nuh-uh," I replied, even though I feared she might be right. I actually tried justifying the learning aspect and talked up the inexpensive housing that would allow me to explore the city on a budget. Yet, the night before I left, she somehow predicted imminent behavior of the moronic kind. Her parting words: "Don't act like an idiot and remember how many calories there are in alcohol."

A week after settling into my two-star hotel room, I'd become friends with a couple of girls in the program, Tina-Marie and Sara. Although my new buds were half my age they remarked that I could "totally pass for thirty," and I stupidly started to believe it. My energy was boundless. My thirst to drink up that potent city and relive my younger days became a literal interpretation. (Gunning for perpetually intoxicated seemed about right.)

One day the three of us were strolling around St. Germain. We stopped in front of a shop and the slutty display brought back fond memories from my '80s punk rock phase.

"Too bad I can't wear shoes like that anymore," I said to my pals with nonexistent pores.

"Honey, you should. You're *still* hot," Tina-Marie quipped.

I hate it when someone says that. It makes me think of a chicken that's been taken out of the oven and left on the counter, but might still be edible. Even though the time limit for actual hotness has passed, its lukewarm state could be overlooked by the truly starving.

Tina-Marie and Sara dragged me in amongst the stacks of shoeboxes. Maybe it was Paris, maybe it was the umpteen Kir Royales I'd consumed, or maybe it was the fact I was shopping with twenty-four year olds? I'm not quite sure, but I spied a pair of metallic t-strapped five-inch platforms and slapped them on. I caught a glimpse of knotted calf in the mirror.

"You HAVE to get those!" they both shrieked.

I teetered around the boutique trying to recall the last time I'd worn heels so high. Oh, right. How could I forget that wasted night at Nell's, in pleather vintage boots designed solely for leaning against a brick wall in a dark alley, or anything that did not involve walking. I sprained my ankle so badly, the next day my foot looked like a meatloaf.

Yet, the optimism in the girls' eyes led me to believe I could pull them off.

"O.K.," I agreed. *Why the hell not?*

"You should totally wear those tonight," the girls chimed in unison.

For some stupid-ass reason, I'd also packed a Victoria's Secret push-up bra I'd bought the year before to appease the guy I was dating after he'd pointed at Tyra Banks' cleavage during *America's Next Top Model* and grunted, "I like." Jesus. Whatever possessed me to Kardashian-up is unknown, but somehow I figured the hoisting of the boobs went nicely with the hooker heels. A plunging v-neck dress completed my new persona. I could have been a living ad for a doll named "Menopausal Cougar Barbie" (Detachable paunch sold separately).

It reminded me of when I used to trade tops with some prettier friend in Junior High. Back then I thought sporting a disguise would lead to a better, zit-free life. The idea of donning another girl's threads was moderately thrilling and usually lasted until somebody complimented her for wearing *my* blouse.

Later at a crowded, hipster brasserie with the rankest unisex toilet in Western Europe, our trio kicked back under an awning and naturally ordered more drinks. Underneath the glimmering streetlights, there he stood, a swizzle-stick in a dirty suit, smoking a long, brown cigarette. He looked majorly cool in his too-tight jacket, like the dude from *Twilight*, only without the pallid skin tone.

"He's totally checking you out," said Tina-Marie.

"Oh, yeah, sure," I laughed.

He flicked his cigarette butt onto the wet cobblestones and sauntered over to our table. His arrogant eyes locked with mine. But, as he moved closer, his B.O. reeked more than the bathroom's stench, if that was possible. I quickly rose with an attempt to gasp fresher air and fell forward knocking my purse off an empty chair. My drunk-ass scramble caused my legs to wobble like a newborn colt on coke. I always wondered if I could still do the splits.

"From a deestance, I thought your mother waz one of those housewives from your American television," he said in broken English, looking at Sara.

If only I'd learned the French translation for "Blow me." I should have kicked that stinky prick upside the

Balzac. But, technically he was right. Forgetting your age can often backfire. And it felt just as shitty as the first time some Jack-wad called me "Ma'am."

I quietly limped off into the darkness and hailed a taxi back to the hotel, which seemed to be the most non-idiotic thing I'd done since arriving in Paris. I'm pretty sure I called my mom and bitched about the eight-pound weight gain situation, but maturely blamed it on the baked goods.

Jill Paris is a writer living in Los Angeles. She holds an M.A. in Humanities and a Master of Professional Writing degree from the University of California. Her work has appeared in The Best Travel Writing 2009, Travel Africa *magazine,* The Saturday Evening Post, Wanderlust & Lipstick, Fathom, Thought Catalog *and others. She travels for the unexpectedness of human connection.*

Mt. Fuji in a Trash Bag

A hiker finds her power in reverse.

"Pack warm clothes it's going to be cold. I checked the weather reports; it's supposed to rain," Jen warns me. *Cold? It's the middle of July.* As I lie on the floor in only my underwear, soaking in a bath of my own sticky sweat, it's hard to imagine putting anything resembling "warm clothes" on my body. Summertime in Tokyo is a sweltering nightmare of mind-bending heat and humidity. Sweaters have become my enemy; they are currently being held prisoner under my bed where I don't have to see them and be reminded of their wooliness. Also, there isn't a whole lot of room for storage in the teeny tiny box the school I'm working for calls an apartment.

"I've heard reports of a monsoon. There's supposed to be gale force winds," Jen adds.

I'm not exactly sure how forceful a gale is, but deciding to heed Jen's advice I toss a couple long sleeved t-shirts and an extra pair of socks into my backpack. On my way to Shinjuku Station I pop into a 99 yen store, buy myself a plastic raincoat and think, *yeah, that should do it!*

"I'm cold," I shiver miserably at the base camp of Mt. Fuji after I've layered every bit of clothing I could get my hands on.

"I told you it would be cold," Jen says not very sympathetic to my plight.

"How was I supposed to know there'd be snow? Who's ever heard of snow in July?"

Mt. Fuji is only open to the public during the months of July and August as the weather is too severe any other time of the year. Apparently monsoon season doesn't rank high on the weather severity chart for the The Japanese. These real hikers view climbing Fuji as a rite of passage that must be honored at some point in their life. For this reason the mountain is teeming with hordes of pilgrimage hungry mountaineers decked out in the finest gear. Teams of them are wearing matching stream-lined snow jackets all branded with some famous mountaineering label, argyle socks stretching to their knees, spring-loaded walking sticks, heat-activated gloves, spiky shoes, hats with lamps, fog proof goggles, and blinking tracking devices in case of an unfortunate tumble off a cliff. I stand, clearly inferior, in a few lumpy mismatched layers and what is essentially a trash bag with armholes masquerading as a raincoat.

"Dave, what else have you got in that bag of yours?" I ask, scavenging for more.

"Just this bottle of champagne."

Dave has been waiting weeks to make his move on Jen, and he's decided this trip is the perfect opportunity. He plans to impress Jen by pulling out the bottle of bubbly, at the top of Japan, as the sun pokes its sleepy head out to awaken the day.

"You got that champagne from the 99 yen store, it was next to my coat. Classy." I give him a look that says, *good luck with that buddy.*

"Here." Dion says offering me an extra hoodie.

Dion didn't have anything better to do, which is how he came to be the fourth member of our not so stylish, nor adequately prepared, Japanese expat mountain climbing team.

Most people, not us people, begin the 12,388 feet ascent at around ten o'clock in the evening. This allows time to hike throughout the night and arrive at the summit in time for the sunrise. We decide to start at eight, which will give us a nice head start from the crowd and allow us to travel at a leisurely pace. Jen takes the lead and Dave eagerly trots along after her. Dion and I hold up the rear enjoying the relative serenity and surprising ease of the trail.

"How come we're not going uphill? Isn't that the point of climbing a mountain?" I ask.

"Sometimes, depending on how the trail is made, you have to go down before you start going up," Dion answers, somewhat unconvinced with his own reasoning.

I choose to believe his sound logic. I like this kind of non-strenuous hiking. After about an hour though it's becoming more evident that we are traveling in the wrong direction. It becomes obvious when we hit a paved highway, the very highway that led us to base camp in the first place.

Two hours later we find ourselves back at the beginning. We set off again, but now we are amongst the horde and this time it's hard. I had envisioned a wooded trail with forest critters and the hoots of the old night owl to serenade our quest. It turns out that when you get this high nothing grows and the trail is just a zigzagging straight up climb through rock, gravel and dirt. If you could see the line of people making their way up the narrow path it would have looked like one great, impossibly slow-moving exodus, like one of those biblical epics where the persecuted are always being exiled from their hallowed land.

You couldn't actually see though because the rumored monsoon finally hit rendering visibility nil.

A strong gust of wind rips me from my holy fantasy and takes my dollar raincoat with it. I clutch a large boulder as to not suffer the same fate. The wind lets up for a brief spell, allowing me to stumble from my rocky refuge and resume my crawl to the peak. I hear nothing but the whooshing sound of wind rushing through my ears. I can see even less. We are shrouded in a cocoon of fog, mist and rain. After what feels like hours, we stumble upon an oddly located tin urinal and the four of us clamber inside hoping for a respite from the elements.

"I'm not going any further," Jen declares sliding to the floor hugging her knees to her chest.

"I'm staying with Jen," Dave says falling to the floor beside her, content with this arrangement.

"Who would build a toilet here?" Dion muses.

It was never my plan to hike Mt. Fuji. I had come along solely because Jen had suggested it over a few beers last week and I'd thought it would be a cool thing to be able to tell people. *Fuji, yeah, done that.* For some reason though I'm overcome with an intense and burning desire to finish what we've set out to accomplish.

"Come on guys we can do it!" I rally as if I'd swallowed a cheerleader on my way up.

"I spent twenty-one days hiking the Annapurna Circuit in Nepal at heights of 17,000 feet, without a Sherpa. This is worse." Jen responds shooting me an icy glare.

"Well I'm gonna do it. We're already over halfway there. Who's with me?" I look around expectantly.

Dion snuggles closer to Jen.

"Oh, all right," sighs Dion, "Let's do it."

Dion and I continue on for I don't know how long; time being yet another victim of the freezing cold. My eyes sting and burn with the little bits of dirt and debris that fly into them. Running on adrenaline, I want to surge forward but I can't. I'm stuck in a traffic jam of pilgrims and suffering the worst kind of pedestrian rage. You always hear mountain climbers extol the virtues of their passion. They speak of the spiritual highs and the soul enriching beauty and peace of the journey.

Mt. Fuji is a bitch and I don't care for her.

Just as I'm cursing her name under my breath we happen upon a cabin, which stops us in our tracks. This must be the top! You build structures at the top of mountains not perched precariously along its edges. I feel a fellow crusader gently tap me on the back.

"No, no my child. Just rest. Still further we must travel," he says with Yoda-esque composure. At least that's what I surmise he is saying, but I can't speak Japanese.

But I don't want to go further. I want to rest. I imagine a kindly hermit woman residing inside tending to her fire. She would bring us piping hot mugs of cocoa and make a cozy bed beside her hearth for us to lie down. After all, anyone who would build such a place must want to aid those on their crusades.

"Thirty dollars." Is all she says.

"What?" We respond. She doesn't seem very welcoming.

"Thirty dollars or you get out."

We have to pay the nasty hermit lady thirty dollars each to sleep on the floor of her hard, cold hut for one hour. There is no hot cocoa. Dion and I huddle for warmth, serenaded not by the crackling blaze of the fire, but by the howling winds that rattle and shake the rickety cabin to its foundation. We must have dozed off for only a few minutes when I feel a sharp jab in my ribs. I open my eyes to find the evil hermit lady kicking me in the side. She kicks Dion too.

"Time over. Out."

Dazed and disoriented we hobble outside to discover that daylight is coming. I sense light on the horizon, but it's still skulking behind the storm. We still can't see anymore than a few feet directly in front of us. We must be close but I'm torn as to how we should proceed. We've already lost two of our team; somewhere Dave is seducing Jen in a urinal with a bottle of cheap champagne. Dion appears to be losing it, clutching himself tightly and rocking back and forth.

As I contemplate my desire to continue, I realize something. I don't really care if I get to the top. I've never been the type of person to look at a mountain and think, *yeah I should be on top of that.* The view is nice and all, but I think you can get the same effect standing on your sofa looking down over a dollhouse. In times like these I find it best to reassess one's goals. I've only been in Japan a couple of months and I've already had my first encounter with Fuji. Sure, it's been a bit rocky, but it's a good start.

"You wanna get outta here?" I shout to Dion, breaking him from his muttering hysteria. I don't wait for his reply. I'm already twenty steps closer to warm toes and civilization when I hear his jacket rustling behind me. He disturbs a few rocks that roll past me and knock into my heels as if to say, *Who's the bitch now?* I laugh, not defeated but relived as I inch closer towards my newly assessed goal—the bottom of Mt. Fuji.

★

Sarah Katin has been a television host in Korea, professor in Japan, treehouse dweller in Laos, house painter in New Orleans, sangria swiller in Spain, dragon hunter in Indonesia, and fishmonger in Australia. A two-time contributor to The Best Women's Travel Writing series, she has recently retired (pending her success as a Hollywood screenwriter) from her teaching position in South Korea. These days you can find her hard at work on her next screenplay at her L.A. office (the cushy chair by the window at Starbucks) or in Costa Rica bathing baby sloths. You just never can tell about these things.

Flashed in Fallouja

*A human rights volunteer is exposed
to more than war damage.*

BACK WHEN IT WAS JUST ANOTHER ANGRY IRAQI CITY AND
months before it became a major flashpoint in U.S./Iraqi
relations, I toured Fallouja.

I was investigating war damage at a water treatment
plant, several weeks after President Bush's declaration of
"mission accomplished," when a man exposed himself to
me. He had been brushing close against me as I walked
along the narrow sidewalks that separated the water treatment ponds, the folds of his shoulder-to-ankle robe com-
mingling uncomfortably with my long skirt in the 115
degree heat. I pulled my purse in front of me, defensively
elbowing space between us.

Later, while I was interviewing the water district man-
ager about her staff's heroic efforts to keep the water
flowing during the first onslaught of war, this strange man
squatted unobtrusively in a doorway, caught my eye, and
lifted his *dishdasha*, displaying how Allah had been very
generous to him.

I was shocked! *And* awed. Talk about weapons of mass
distraction! What's a white girl in a war zone to do? Being

flashed in Fallouja isn't covered in the human rights' handbook.

I knew from his quietly creepy behavior that he was violating standards. But should I speak up and risk offending my hosts? The town was already pretty edgy. Later that afternoon, I would be warned that Falloujans had vowed "to kill an American a day" in retaliation for the U.S. troops' gunfire exchange with locals who had taken refuge in a school. Schools are revered in Iraq, and our blanketing one with bullets had further ignited this rebellious community.

But I was always taught that bullies bank on us staying politely silent.

"That man exposed himself to me!" I pointed at him as stiffly as he had to me.

My male translator looked at me, confused. This gentle man, whose religious practice kept him from even touching a member of the opposite gender, repeated something in Arabic to the water treatment workers gathered around us. Meanwhile, in the confusion, the exhibitionist had lowered his *dishdasha* and skulked out.

Well, I had no idea I would cause such a stir! Workers ran after the man, mortified that his aberrant behavior might reflect on them. They made such a fuss with their apologies, *I* began to feel guilty.

"It was no big deal," I offered, rolling my eyes. "Really, it was no *big* deal," I lied.

I guess one of the men understood my double-entendre, because he burst out laughing, easing the tension.

We lose so much in war, and humor is right there with truth among the first casualties. Standing in battle-scarred Fallouja, a stranger and I started the rebuilding by bonding over a very worn pun, proving that when we're brave enough to laugh at ourselves, what really gets exposed is our humanity.

★

Kelly Hayes-Raitt was press credentialed by the Jordanian government as she entered Iraq in July 2003, three months after the US-led invasion. She reported live from Baghdad, Fallouja, Hilla and Basra via satellite phone to National Public Radio, KNBC-TV and other news outlets. The recipient of five writing fellowships, she has lived in writing colonies as far-flung as Bialystok, Poland. She is a popular college lecturer and public speaker and divides her time between Los Angeles, CA, and Ajijic, Mexico. She is writing a memoir about her work with refugees and blogs at www.PeacePATHFoundation.org.

Ditching First Impressions

How do you say gutter ball in French?

"I HOPE YOU DON'T MIND," WILNA SAYS CASUALLY, "BUT I invited a friend of mine to the party. She'll be traveling around Europe during that time."

"Of course," I say. "The more the merrier."

We are on the terrace at Wilna's riverside château in the Dordogne region of France. I met Wilna, a convivial South African woman, nearly five years ago while researching a book. We became fast friends and when my book was released, Wilna's home felt like the natural location for a celebration.

"She is very interested in meeting you actually," Wilna continues. "She too writes about food and travel."

When Wilna tells me her is Gwynne Conlyn, shock on my face is as apparent as the freckles. Serendipity by its very definition arrives unexpectedly and it has just careened into me at the dinner table.

I gush about Gwynne's book *Delicious Travels* and tell Wilna it's a dog-eared and well-read kitchen companion at my house, as well as the impetus for my own culinary travel book. That fact that she wrote extensively for magazines and newspapers *and* had her own radio show, added to her magnetism. Turns out Wilna and Gwynne have been friends for nearly twenty years. We marvel at how small the world is and as I feign brave enthusiasm about meeting Gwynne, my heart pounds and grips the inside of my chest as sweat beads under my arms. It's one thing to admire someone from behind a computer screen, but to actually meet your idol in person? All I can think of is the old adage (or maybe it was a fortune cookie), "You never get a second chance to make a first impression." I start to panic.

Luckily I have a month and a long drive from Brussels back to the Dordogne to set the stage for this perfect 'first impression' meeting. With no working radio in my car, my mind reels and images flip rapid fire through my head of well-crafted introductory scenes that play over and over again à la the movie "Groundhog Day." The more I think about it, the more nervous I become.

I rehearse out loud, hoping to quell the nervous ticks in my voice. People shoot me curious looks as they drive by. Understandable since I am alone in the car.

"Hey Gwynne. How's it goin'?" No, that sounds too informal. I have to show some respect.

I purse my lips and lower my chin. "Hello Ms. Conlyn. I'm a *huge* fan." No, too stiff; Too stalker.

"Oh my gosh, I love your book!" I bubble and bob my head side to side. No, definitely not. Way too Hannah Montana.

A barrage of questions fills my head. Should I shake Gwynne's hand? What if my hands are sweaty? Should I greet her with the standard two-cheek kiss common in France? Did they do that in South Africa? What if she thinks I'm too forward?

On a stretch of French highway with nary a house in sight, my idol-meeting wardrobe becomes my top concern. Since it's been peaking at 95 degrees in the Dordogne, a dress and sandals seem the sensible choice. But will I appear over-dressed? Is my pedicure good enough for sandals?

By the time I reach the Dordogne, I am drenched in worry but have decided on a firm handshake (I will wipe my hands on my dress if I need to) followed by an informal first name introduction and a smile. After all, a mutual friend is introducing us. My toes look fine. Wilna and I plan to meet the next day at an open-air market in the medieval village of Issigeac where Gwynne will join us for lunch.

The rural roads of the Dordogne are serpentine and narrow, and even the tiny French cars no bigger than super-sized roller skates barely fit side by side. My beefy, Belgian-plated German car is an obtrusive interloper. It is also packed with items I am planning to drop off at my house in France---beach chairs, a trash can, dishwasher salt, pillows, a coffee maker and other incongruent occupants that, had I been pulled over, might have suggested I was on the lam after having just knocked over a *Carrefour*, the French equivalent of a Wal-Mart.

A few miles from Issigeac, I roll down my windows to let in the warmth of the sun and allow the air to coif my hair and billow my confidence. I have on a new dress, my nerves are calm and I have rehearsed in my head, ad nauseam, the meeting with Gwynne. It's perfect.

As I round a blind curve on what seems to be a narrower than normal route, I see a large Mercedes truck barreling toward me. It has been gaining speed on a straightaway that stretches out behind it and wasn't slowing down. I immediately take my foot off the gas and maneuver the car to the right. I assume the truck driver will see this and courteously move to his right too, allowing us to pass one another safely. The truck stays its course, speeding down the middle of the road.

My car is now balancing along a tightrope of gravel that separates the asphalt from a two-feet deep drainage ditch that parallels the road. Much like a bowler does after hurling a ten-pound ball toward the pins at the end of a slick lane, I lean and contort my limbs and body to the left, naively assuming I can will my car to do the same and avoid the ditch. But this is no game. I have two choices—a strike, (great in bowling but not so fun in driving) or a gutter ball. I take the gutter ball. Hell, I AM the gutter ball. My car topples almost gracefully in and gradually slows against the heavy dirt and grass until the front tire hits a cement pipe from somewhere underneath the road. A gruesome crunch brings me to a sudden and slanted stop.

I am fine (the airbag didn't even deploy) but my car isn't going anywhere. I look around for my cell phone but can't find it. Several items that had been neatly stacked on my passenger seat had flown out the window and I can see them splayed like a yard sale on the ground outside. I assume my cell phone is among the debris. The angle at which the car has settled makes it difficult, but I manage to heave myself out of the driver's side, and slice my shin on the door the process. My phone has landed at the bottom of the ditch, damp from water that has come, presumably, from that blasted cement pipe. I step in to grab it and my foot squishes into the soggy dirt. As I sink, the mud belches out a steady slurp reminiscent of a straw sucking the bottom of an empty glass. Mud oozes between my toes and sandal. I half expect Ashton Kutcher to jump from behind a bush and tell me I'm being "punked." Instead, a woman is walking toward me. She says she was working in her garden when the truck sped by and she had heard the subsequent crash.

"Where is the truck?" she asks.

"It never came back."

"Then they are not French. A French person would have stopped," she says, wagging her index finger back and forth.

I smile at her defense of her countrymen. The French are so proud.

I ask her if she will call a *dépanneuse,* a word that means both tow truck and wrecker in French. Obviously I have already taken care of the latter. I call Wilna with my mucky phone and tell her I will not be joining them for lunch.

"I'll come wait with you," she comforts, "and then we can go together."

Vanity whispers in my ear and I think of my bloody leg and my sweat-stained dress, accessorized by a sandal caked in mud, and of course the filthy phone print that's now on my face. There is no way I can meet Gwynne looking like this.

"No, no," I insist. "I'll just have the driver take me to his garage and will call a taxi."

"Where do you think you are, New York City?" Wilna retorts. "There are no taxis here."

Point taken. And so I wait by the side of the road like the proverbial damsel in distress, only I'm armed with a cell phone, which definitely helps matters. I wonder how many cartoon women could have been rescued from the railroad tracks had their animators drawn in an iPhone.

Several people (all French) stop to make sure help is on the way and inquire just how exactly I had managed to plow my car into a ditch. Among them an older couple, both wearing matching concerned looks beneath their white hair, that want to try and dislodge my car by pushing on the front fender. I discourage them and send them on their way. A young man on a motorcycle also stops. I'm tempted, only for a minute, to ride off with him and forget this whole mess.

The noon sun blazes down on me. I can feel my shoulders burning and my mascara mixing with sweat and streaking my face. From my packed trunk, now a jumble of clothes, coffee grounds and dishwasher salt, I manage to pluck out an umbrella, which I use to provide some shade. Eventually a black four-door car pulls up in front of me. I don't recognize it as Wilna's but she emerges from the passenger side door. And out of the driver's side steps a blond woman wearing a coral colored dress and a red-lipstick smile. Oh no.

I quickly wipe my sweaty hand on my dress. At least that part of my plan remains intact. There is no hope for my gooey shoe. "And nothing breaks the ice like a bloody leg," I think to myself, trying to bolster my deflated ego. I return the smile and feel the dirt and mascara crack on my face.

The blond woman extends her hand.

"Hi. I'm Gwynne."

Before I can introduce myself she says,

"You look like you could use a beer."

She reaches down into her shoulder bag and pulls out a Stella Artois.

"I figured Belgian would be your preference," she says.

Gwynne pops the cap and hands me the cold bottle.

Feeling happy, calm and completely myself, I share with Gwynne my admiration of her book and she asks about mine. We talk about our other travel mishaps and laugh like old friends, two South Africans and an American huddled under an umbrella, sipping Belgian beer and waiting for my German car to be pulled from a ditch in the French countryside.

It's exactly the first impression I had hoped to make.

★

Kimberley Lovato is a freelance travel and lifestyle journalist. Her writing has appeared in AFAR, National Geographic, Traveler, Executive Travel, Easy Jet Travel, *the* San Francisco Chronicle, *and online at frommers.com and Leite's Culinaria. Her culinary travel book* Walnut Wine & Truffle Groves *about the Dordogne region of France was released in 2010 and has won two awards. Her essay, "Lost and Liberated," was published in* The Best Women's Travel Writing, Volume 8. *Visit her at kimberleylovato.com.*

JULIAN WORKER

Safari Sickness

*He had avoided illnesses caused by microscopic
organisms but then took a ride on the largest
land animal in the world.*

THE WORD "SAFARI" BRINGS TO MIND THE OPEN SAVANNAH
with vast tracts of blue sky, giraffes eating the tops of trees,
lions lying on a low mound observing their prey, and
herds of zebras trotting across the plain. For me, however,
the word conjures a queasy feeling. Safari means motion
sickness, being showered with stream water, and oxygen
deprivation.

I had traveled for five weeks in India and managed to
stay free of illness the whole time. I put this down to luck
more than anything, though drinking four liters of water
a day to stay hydrated is definitely a good policy for any
visitor. But somehow, as I crossed the border into Nepal,
I had a feeling my luck would change. The first inkling
came when I realized that Nepal is actually fifteen minutes
ahead of Indian time. My first day was spent assuming all
the clocks were wrong and that seeing the airport bus dis-
appearing into the distance and having shop doors locked
and bolted in my face were unfortunate coincidences.

On my second day, with my watch set correctly after checking with the hotel concierge, I headed to Chitwan National Park to go on safari. This was going to be a special day spent on the back of an elephant looking for rhinos. However, my luck was about to change. There was a shortage of elephants and so we tourists had to go four per elephant plus the mahout on the animal's back. In other words, there was a tourist at each corner of the elephant, not that our animal seemed to mind as he was a large beast with the most enormous expressive green eyes. Our mahout welcomed us onboard his elephant, whose name was Major. We were given our pre-flight instructions, which essentially were to hang on and make sure that we didn't fall off. We had to keep our feet braced against a rope hanging from the animal's saddle and we all sat with another rope looped around us.

After we settled down, the mahout shouted "Major Go" and the elephant departed in search of rhinos. It quickly became apparent that the elephant was very heavy-footed and every foot placement was a shock to the system. He also had one leg that seemed shorter than the others so that he had a rolling gait, which may seem funny but it meant that not only was I being shocked but there was a circular motion which gradually induced motion sickness in me.

After ten minutes Major felt hungry and so stopped and ate a large bush in three trunkfuls. Mercifully, my queasiness eased as Major ate brunch. The driver informed us that Major usually ate around 100 pounds of vegetative matter per day, a very high-fiber diet. We were soon off again and the rolling and shocking started again.

Soon Major was thirsty, so he headed for a small stream and sucked up a ten-yard stretch in a matter of seconds. As an encore he raised his trunk vertically in the air and blew out the last two yards of water so that we tourists were treated to our own mini-monsoon. He trumpeted slightly. He was happy, we weren't.

Major was off again. After five minutes he stopped once more and this time he raised his tail vertically. What goes in must eventually come out especially with a high-fiber diet. The stench was horrible though I managed to hold my breath for the whole time. However, Major stayed in the same spot after finishing as though he was savoring the occasion and so I had to breathe in this horrible smell. There wasn't much oxygen around and I began to feel sick; luckily Major moved and some fresh air entered my lungs saving me . . . for the moment.

The mahout spotted a rhino and off we went at a trot, with the circular motion now giving me a headache. Major stopped abruptly five yards from the rhino, who'd had his horn cut off by the park authorities to save him from poachers. Major was wary of the rhino who sniffed the air suspiciously before continuing to eat.

After ten minutes admiring the rhino we trotted away and entered a jungle clearing. The air was perfectly still. Major stopped again. A profound gurgling came from inside the elephant and he lifted his tail again. This time he broke wind for longer than I could hold my breath. I suffered from oxygen deprivation and the methane entered my lungs, making me gag.

My luck has taken a huge turn for the worse, I thought, being gassed on the back of an elephant—who would have thought it possible? I had avoided illnesses caused by microscopic organisms on holiday and here I was being made ill by the largest land animal in the world. The irony wasn't totally lost on me as my head lolled on my chest as we headed back to our base. I felt nauseous, had a bad headache, and knew I was going to be sick. I crawled off Major, smiled wanly at the mahout, and almost made it back to my cabin.

The doctor came to see me and thought I might have cholera. He ignored my weak excuses that I had been gassed on the back of an elephant; he said being slightly delirious was a sign of possible cholera and told me to stay in bed for the rest of the day.

The following day I was fine but when I was offered another safari I politely declined.

So, if you ever go into the bush on an elephant, do sit at the front, and if possible measure its legs just to make sure they are all the same length.

Julian Worker has written on architecture for the U. S. maga-zine Skipping Stones *and had travel articles published* in The Globe and Mail, Fate Magazine, The Vancouver Sun, *and* Northwest Travel. *He blogs about travel on the* In The Know Traveler *website and his work has appeared online on the* World and I, Offbeat Travel, *and* GoNomad *websites. He has also taken many photographs that have appeared in travel guides by* National Geographic, Thomas Cook and The Rough Guides. *India is his favorite country as a travel destination.*

Meeting Mosquito

She'd always wanted to face her fear of heights—
and hang-gliding in Rio allowed her to
scratch that itch.

AFTER THE RAGING LUNATIC THAT WAS LAST NIGHT'S THUN-
derstorm, louder and longer than any we see in New York
City, the Hilton Fly Rio Hang Gliding Center would
undoubtedly shelve our excursion. At least, that's what
the concierge at our Rio de Janeiro hotel had explained.
So I choked down another greasy piece of bacon, another
spoonful of sour plain yogurt, savored piece after piece of
candy-sweet pineapple until I slumped over in my seat at
the breakfast buffet. I glanced down at my Chicago Bears
t-shirt, which I'd specifically chosen for a day where the
odds that I would die were greater than most.

When your parents are as openly acrophobic as mine, you
grow up convinced that you're also acrophobic. Together my
husband Jeff and I had surfed, speed-biked down volcanoes,
gone scuba diving with sharks as big as sofas, eels, manta
rays, and barracuda. But it was no accident that I'd never
agreed to adventures involving dizzying heights. That's why
I was puzzled to overhear him telling some new friends:
"Hang gliding? Yeah! Sure, we'd love to!"

I knew hang-gliding was a tourist tradition in Rio—since the mid-1970s I'd later learn—with nearly 10,000 tandem flights each year. I've never been one to decline a challenge, and this felt like a triple-dog dare. Jeff took me aside to coax. I ultimately conceded. And, instead of my memories flashing before me in a quick-but-painless final instant, I was blessed with hours of panicked reflection in a single sleepless night.

My anxiety, however, was unjustified; after all, this storm would be my savior—or so I thought.

The sliding glass doors of the hotel entryway brushed open and closed as we waited. And then, to our surprise, my dismay, it coasted into the scene: the secret-service-like SUV that would transport us to a 1,700-foot-high hilltop in the depths of Floresta da Tijuca, the world's largest urban forest. I felt the Ipanema tan drain from my face.

"Too much breeze for you back there?" Jeff asked our friends. "Though then again, given what we're about to do!" We both crack jokes when we're nervous, and today they were rolling off his tongue like coconuts. Thud. We continued to land-cruise past the Atlantic Ocean waves, clouded with rainwater and twisted with sand. I squinted and spotted what looked like a toy hang-glider floating in the distance. I reached for his hand.

The vehicle swerved subtly as our driver's eyes left the road to turn around and introduce himself. But all we understood through his thick Portuguese accent was his nickname: Mosquito. Jeff spouted, "'Mosquito,' really? That's the best you could do? How about Eagle? Or Hawk? Or . . . ."

"All right, funny man, that oughta do it," I interrupted.

Mosquito chattered for the remaining twenty minutes of our drive. "We make dreams come true," he pitched. "You want to fly like a bird? We help you fly like a bird!"

He amused himself with the story of an eighty-four-year-old client: "See? Anyone can do it!"

"Mosquito, would you please turn on the radio? I need some music to get pumped for our jump," I requested sarcastically feeling more than a touch of bacon-and- anxiety-induced nausea. Anything to drown out his transparent "don't back out now" sales speech. We hadn't paid him yet.

He cranked some Samba. "But is not a jump!" he scolded. "Never jump. You must run. Your pilot will explain." The tires crunched as we wound our way up and up and up a narrow, gravel mountain road. And Mosquito rambled on about Rio's pure air.

When we disembarked on a dusty plateau with a make-shift snack bar, I smelled the stagnant sewage from the out-of-service "sanitarios." A crowd was gathered on bleachers built into the cliff, and their roof was a fifteen-foot-long ramp of two-by-four floorboards leading off into that pure air. "All the better to trip you with, my dear," I muttered. I may be athletic, but I'm also clumsy.

Staff members yanked each member of our group in different directions. Rony, my tandem pilot in a bright orange shirt and over-gelled, spiky, black hair, stepped me into the thin, cloth, armless straightjacket that would clip me to what's essentially an oversized kite. He and I sprinted back and forth together to simulate takeoff, as if we were competing in a three-legged race.

"You will run as fast as you can, yes?" he insisted.

I nodded.

"No nod. Promise," he insisted.

"I promise." My stomach churned—yogurt, pineapple and all. Any remaining saliva in my dry mouth tasted metallic.

I wasn't sure how it happened so quickly but, in my peripheral vision, I saw Jeff in ready position at the top of the wooden runway.

"I love you!" I shouted as if it would be the last time. He glared back at me as if this had been my idea, not his. I watched my husband disappear into the clouds.

"Ready?" my pilot asked. "We must hurry before the weather turns."

Before the weather turns? I realized that the helmet fasten didn't hug my chin.

"Is this safe?" I asked as I showed him the gap between strap and skin.

He responded only with a laugh, led me to the ledge and instructed me to keep my left hand on his back and my right hand on a noose hanging from the steering bar at all times. His back sweat on my left hand. The frayed khaki rope splintered in my right.

"And . . . RUN!" he yelled.

My legs sloshed like water balloons; they weren't my own. I couldn't keep up with him. But when we reached the edge, there was no drop—of jaw, of stomach, of limp, freefalling body. We were flying, as promised, like an eagle, a hawk . . . a mosquito. I gasped. Besides my pilot's breathing, my breathing and my babbling internal stream of consciousness, all I heard was . . . nothing. The wind silently echoed in my cold ears. I started to notice details in the Brazilian landscape that I couldn't possibly have seen from sea level. I wished I could swap out my smelly pilot and swap in Jeff. Or better yet, enjoy my flight in solitude.

That inner peace lasted about a minute until it hit me: more than 1,000 feet between me and the unforgiving ground. That's all. Rony repeatedly clicked a button with his thumb and grinned into a camera at the front right edge of our kite. I gave it dirty looks.

Are the clips holding me to the glider made of metal or plastic? What if they forgot about one of the clips altogether? What would I do if I heard the sound of splitting fabric or tearing Velcro? Could I hold my full body weight from this thin rope and, if I could, what would happen during landing? LANDING? We never even discussed landing!

I remembered reading once that bird bones are hollow; human bodies aren't built to fly. As we circled, I didn't feel weightless; I felt every ounce of my mass, multiplied. It pushed against the material of my straightjacket as if I were as large and dense as a Chicago Bears linebacker. Brian Urlacher. Refrigerator Perry even.

Would it be better if I were to plummet into that block of trees over there? Into the pool behind that mansion? Into the ocean? Is it true that your body goes into shock during free fall—that you don't feel the pain of impact? Would it be quicker if we crashed into a cliff?

Without warning, over the same Atlantic Ocean waves we'd driven past earlier, my pilot ripped off my leg straps. My feet dangled with awkward freedom.

"Again, you will run. Stand up very straight," he coached.

He pulled back and, as our speed slowed, we hovered over the shoreline.

Touchdown!

Jeff, also grateful for solid ground, proudly waved to me from the shade of a nearby palm tree. I wobbled, then felt a manic rush of adrenaline, and we swapped stories. His pilot had taken four cell phone calls—in flight—and their out-of-control beach landing had involved a gritty tumble. But he loved it.

"I'm really proud of the bragging rights, but I can't imagine doing it again," I confessed.

"Come on, you wouldn't?" he prodded.

Are we mere men, or are we mosquito? I asked myself. I flashed back to the spectacular sight of Rio de Janeiro from above in all its glory—the mountains, the mansions, the ocean, the favelas, forest, beach—and I couldn't come up with a better way to take in the sweeping view. I caught a glimpse of the next aircraft approaching the sand.

That was me. I did that. Maybe I don't have a fear of heights after all. Or maybe I do, but I'm brave enough to face it. Yes. I would do it again. I am mosquito.

Josey Miller is on-camera and voiceover talent, a singer-songwriter, and a respected travel and lifestyle journalist. Her travel writing credits include the New York Times, *the* Los Angeles Times, *the* Washington Post, Time Out New York *magazine,* The Nest *magazine,* Concierge.com, Epicurious.com, *and BBC Travel. She lives in the West Village of New York City with her husband, Jeff, their son, Mason, and their cats, Gray and Benji. Learn more at joseymiller.com.*

JILL K. ROBINSON

Wasted in Margaritaville

A bad trip can be made better with tequila.

I ALMOST DIDN'T TAKE THIS TRIP. THE IDEA OF TRAVELING around Mexico's tequila country in a van, drinking from morning until well, morning, seemed the type of vacation I should have taken in my 20s. But after a few margaritas one night, I listened to the stories of friends who had gone the previous year, and my curiosity got the better of me. Had I known that I'd spend the trip imagining how to knock off two of my fellow travelers and make it look like an unfortunate accident, I might have reconsidered.

There were nine of us on the weeklong trip touring distilleries: Julio (our well-connected leader), Paco (our sober driver) and seven fans of tequila. While we'd been friends with Julio for years, many of us had only just met each other. Drinking began after we checked in at our hotel in Guadalajara and from there on, only stopped for sleep and breakfast. Needless to say, breakfast consisted of quiet, non-crunchy fare. Due to Julio's friendships in the liquor industry, the week was a unique blur of food, tequila and distilleries. The flood of food and drink seemed to be endless. Meals provided by our distillery hosts were banquets with options beyond the corner taqueria: smoky chipotle carne asada combined with the creamy texture of spicy guacamole, green-bean tasting nopales (cactus) and sweet grilled green onions were additions to warm corn handmade tortillas, crispy chicharrones were served with earthy black beans and sharp cheese. All were washed down with crisp, oaky tequila.

On the first day, I was already prepared to toss one couple off the trip. The trouble began after a tour and tequila tasting at Pueblo Viejo, in the Arandas region of the Mexican state of Jalisco. We sat down to lunch with our hosts in a saloon-style building, complete with swinging doors. As the entire table toasted each other, Sally saluted our friend who had taken us on the trip. "To Julio," she slurred. "To Julio's margaritas. You'd probably have to blow him to get the recipe." Our more modest distillery friends stared at their plates. Everyone else stared at Sally.

An hour later, after a failed trip through the swinging doors resulted in Sally falling face down after the door hit her in the backside on the way out, she passed out on the edge of a fountain shaped like a shot glass. Her mouth gaped open, as if she expected the glass to tip and offer her more tequila. Her arms were stretched over her head, pulling tightly on her black, too short dress. The wind had blown her skirt up over her stomach, giving us a view of not just her black lacy underwear. That was Sally, always charming.

We said goodbye to our hosts near the Sally fountain. Each time I spoke to someone, I tried to maneuver them so that they were facing away from the view. I didn't want to be remembered as that woman who was on the trip with the drunken exhibitionist.

In the van on the way to the next distillery, I passed around one of several bottles of tequila that we'd been given by our new friends at Pueblo Viejo. There were no cups, so my husband pulled out his pocketknife and deftly cut our empty water bottles in half and I began to pour. Sally and her boyfriend, Todd, quickly turned up the volume on a spat that had apparently begun in the morning.

"I should have known better than to let you hold the watch. You're so irresponsible," said Todd, his voice already tequila-foggy. His skinny frame was folded into the back corner of the van.

"I didn't lose it. It's here somewhere. Besides, it's too expensive a watch for you to take on vacation," retaliated Sally, who was propping herself up against one of the tinted windows, which gave her pasty skin a tinge of green.

"You're already drunk. It's disgusting. I know you lost the watch, you bitch. Why don't you just admit it?"

"Bitch? I'm a bitch? You asshole. Get away from me!"

Todd snatched Sally's half-full glass of tequila from her, sloshing the liquid across the back seat, while the rest of us sneaked glances at each other and rolled our eyes hard enough to affect the tides. If they fought like this every day, it would be a long and painful trip.

The fight wore on through our next distillery visit, and by dinnertime, they weren't speaking to each other. I was amazed it had taken them *that* long. Sally sulked back at the hotel, and Todd accompanied us to the first ten minutes of dinner, until he slumped in his chair and had to be carried back to the hotel. Sally insisted they stay in separate rooms.

By breakfast, it seemed as if the fight was forgotten. Todd wore his watch on his tanned wrist, and nobody said a word about its sudden appearance.

In the van that day, I thought of a plan to avoid another painful day of fighting. I admit, I briefly considered dosing their food or drink with something to make them sleep, but a quick survey of the other travelers turned up only the relatively harmless Advil and Imodium. I turned to Plan B. Since Sally and Todd were already driving me crazy and they seemed to lack the talent of spacing their drinking out through the day to avoid getting hammered before dinner, I had decided to get rid of them early. I poured a small amount of tequila in everyone's water bottle cup except their two cups, which I nearly filled. They were sitting up near the front of the van this time, so they didn't notice the difference. The small amounts were finished quickly.

"Come on, you drink too slow. Look, we're already finished." I held up my empty cup to illustrate, and Sally and Todd quickly chugged their tequila and offered their cups for a refill—which I provided gladly. I relied on their competitive nature and figured they would want to match what they perceived to be everyone's level of drinking.

I ignored the stares from my fellow travelers, knowing that they'd approve of my scheme when I got a chance to explain myself. It was harder to ignore the elbow in my ribs and angry glare courtesy of my husband. "I'm putting them down *early*," I whispered to him, hoping he'd be discreet in passing the word around. After a while, I noticed the smiles and winks of appreciation. I hoped my plan would work.

That day, Sally and Todd passed out before dinner, and I was thankful for such a simple secret weapon. Too much tequila for them allowed the rest of us to finally enjoy ourselves. Unfortunately, word of the plan hadn't gotten around to everyone quickly enough, and my friend Robert was lost by dinnertime as well. I spent every day for the rest of the trip making sure that Sally and Todd had full glasses so that we could delight in our evenings without their company—and I could avoid a Mexican prison.

★

Jill K. Robinson is a freelance writer and editor. Her work has appeared in the San Francisco Chronicle, World Hum, Journey, *Lonely Planet, Frommer's and more. When she's not traveling, she's at home in El Granada, California, or Guanaja, Honduras. She'd prefer to drink good tequila than use it as a weapon.*

Cabin Pressure

Her tank was full. Her options empty.

THE PRESSURE HAD BEEN BUILDING FOR HOURS. MY HANDS gripped the grey wheel of the Citroën until my knuckles were white. A clammy sweat lay heavily on my forehead. Fat raindrops mocked me as they flowed across the windshield. I had been driving through the French countryside since morning. And I had to pee like nobody's business.

The day had begun serenely enough. I was midpoint in an eight-day trek that sliced back and forth across southwest France, starting near the Atlantic coast at Bordeaux and heading east to the Perigord Noir and the castle-strewn land of the Dordogne River.

I had spent the night at a comfortable stone farmhouse after a day touring the medieval village of Saint-Émilion, an oenophile's dream of rich red wines. In the morning, I filled up on the ubiquitous baguette, butter, and homemade jam of French bed and breakfasts, and then stepped outside, eager for another day of solo travel. A light mist covered the landscape, and diffused sunshine gave the lime green vineyards a fuzzy glow.

After breathing in the cool morning air, I reached for the door of the grey sedan. Just as any mom will appreciate a hotel room—"I don't have to make the bed!"—or a restaurant meal—"I don't have to do the dishes!"—so I appreciated this rental car, where, clearly, no child had ever kicked muddy sneakers against the back of the driver's seat, nor dropped greasy fries that would be discovered in crevices years later, nor left a red crayon that would permanently melt into the fabric seat cover in the summer's heat. As I entered the immaculate black interior, I felt happy and free—or as free as a mother of two can be. It helps to put an ocean between you and your kids.

With a bottle of Evian and maps, and I was ready for the long drive to my next destination. It was a mild fall morning and the scenery was picturesque. First there were acres of vineyards, long straight rows of green across softly arching stretches of land. Then orchards, where ripe plums just lay on the ground. I pulled over and grabbed a few off the wet grass. After rinsing one with my bottled water, I took a bite. The taught blackish-purple skin snapped under my teeth and my mouth filled with sweet juice. Now this was road food!

My route wound its way through numerous old villages. I was fascinated by a church whose stone façade was cut like a lace doily. A half dozen bells dangled on it like showy earrings on a cabaret singer. I stopped and took some photos. This was what I loved about driving as opposed to train or plane travel—the opportunities for discovery, the ability to pause and soak it all in.

After the first hour, a heavy rain began, and I got serious about driving safely on the slick foreign roads. And then I felt it. The first twinges of the need to relieve myself.

While Europe's countrysides possess numerous charms, convenience is not among them. Deep in the country, I knew there would be no public restrooms for miles, so I soldiered on, fiddling to tune in NRJ—the French radio station that reliably pumped out bass-thumping dance hits.

Finally, the two-lane road grew to four, and the farms and vineyards gave way to factories and outlet stores. I pulled into the parking lot of a supermarché. Inside, I searched the perimeter of the store, walking with that hip-twitching gait that comes with trying to hold it in. Tracking down an employee, I inquired about the restroom in French.

Asking for the bathroom is one of the most essential language skills of foreign travel, right up there with being able to say yes and no. I can ask for the bathroom in French, "Où est la toilette?" Italian, "Dove il gabinetto?" If I don't know how to say "Where is," I can simply use the word for bathroom and inflect my voice up while raising my eyebrows, such as "Baño?" in Spanish.

The woman flatly replied, "La clé est perdue." The key is lost. I wanted to ask her, "How does this happen? How do you lose a bathroom key and never replace it or change the lock?" I wanted to grab her by her loose red supermarket shirt and shake her thin French shoulders and say, "But where do you go to the bathroom?" Instead, I retreated from the store, promptly setting off a high-pitched alarm as I removed a fabric band blocking a closed checkout lane. I walked as fast as possible—considering it would be less embarrassing to run—and returned to my car: spirits low, bladder full.

The drive continued and my anxiety increased. I desperately wanted to pull over and run behind a tree. But the roads were frustratingly barren of any vegetation higher than my kneecap.

As I drove, my eyes darted back and forth, scanning both sides of the road for any sign of a toilet. And then I saw a dull concrete block of a building. "Yes!" I whipped my car into a small parking lot, where three male gendarmes were standing around smoking. I ignored them and went into the damp building whose once white stucco walls were now peeling and yellowed. The esthetics were secondary, however. What mattered was that I had succeeded in my quest.

My feeling of euphoria vanished as I walked into a small stall area and found a Turkish toilet: a hole as big as a coffee can with a porcelain surround. I remember being shocked by this seedy answer to nature's call as a young woman of twenty-one on my first trip to Paris. However, it was far better than nothing, so I pulled down my tan travel trousers and squatted. Ahhh . . . the undeniable pleasure of release.

I tossed the tissue into the hole, zipped my pants, then turned around to flush. There was a metal water tank above my head with a pull chain. Simple enough. But also, a handwritten sign on a piece of notebook paper taped to it. "Tirez doucement." Pull gently. Okay, that much I knew. There were more French words that I couldn't translate, but I didn't worry about them. I pulled gently on the chain. Nothing happened.

At that point, I had two choices. I could walk away, my urine having gone into the hole, but the used toilet paper still wadded near the top of the bumpy porcelain floor. I opted not to be the "ugly American." I would try again to properly flush this contraption. So, I pulled slightly harder. And then, a gush of water that I can only compare to heading downhill on a Six Flags log flume, shot out of a pipe, filled up the toilet hole, and headed straight up at a perfect angle towards the lower half of my body. In two seconds my pants and legs were soaked with water that had mixed with my pee and the built up bacteria of the Turkish toilet. I screamed.

While I am not a prissy woman, this was unsanitary beyond any situation I had ever personally been involved with. I stood there dumbfounded and paralyzed for two minutes. I had solved one enormous problem—where to

pee? Only to be immediately confronted by another—
what to do after being soaked by toilet water? I took a
deep breath and drew upon every ounce of traveler's savvy
I could muster. I left the building, where the gendarmes
had scattered. I scowled, imagining them laughing at my
scream, and wondered if they stood around hoping for a
good chuckle from hapless tourists who soak themselves.

Pushing that thought aside, I pulled clean jeans, underwear, and socks out of my suitcase, and returned to the
bathroom, where I gave myself an unsatisfactory sponge
bath from paper towels and put on the clothes to continue
on to my destination.

Later that evening I settled into another bed and breakfast. I took a long shower, where I scrubbed every inch of
myself with the mini hotel soap. I washed my pants with
water as hot as would come out of the tap. When I felt
like I was no longer crawling with microbes, I got dressed
in sweatpants and walked to the back of the inn, where
a small refrigerator held a box of wine. I poured myself
a plastic cup of inexpensive Merlot and returned to sit
on a rattan chair outside of my room. I sipped the fruity
wine and sighed. I saw the black outline of fir trees against
the indigo skies, and I heard cattle lowing, just like in the
Christmas carol. As the wine warmed my insides, I forgot
about the day's trials and fell back in love with the French
countryside. This feeling of acceptance and vive la dif-
férence lasted all the way until the next afternoon, when I
lost the rental car and spent two hours learning that every
exit from the walled town of Sarlat looks exactly the same.
But for the moment, as I watched the clouds drift across
the starry country skies, I was once more content in the
pleasures of the road.

★

Diane Letulle is writing a memoir about her journeys in wine country. Her travels have taken her across North America, from Napa Valley to Niagara on the Lake and all over Europe, from Portugal in the west to the Republic of Georgia in the east. Diane writes a blog called Wine Lover's Journal, contributes to numerous wine websites, and teaches wine classes in New Jersey. She recently was a featured presenter at the International Wine Tourism Conference in Perugia, Italy. Diane is the mother of two children, who have learned to tolerate their mother's itinerant ways.

Sometimes a Language Barrier Isn't

If only we could talk like the animals.

DON'T TAKE THIS THE WRONG WAY, BUT IF THERE'S A LAN-guage barrier between you and an elephant, it's probably your fault.

It turns out that elephants, along with having great strength, excellent long-term memory and a talent for being nifty metaphors (the "elephant in the room" being the, well, obvious one), also have the ability to talk to each other through the ground.

Pachyderms can chat using infrasonic sound, frequencies too low for humans to hear, that can carry through air, water, forest, earth and rock—as far as 2.5 miles.

Quite literally, there is no communication barrier among elephants.

While I freely admit my shortcomings in conversing with elephants, I am a little thankful for the language barrier considering what I imagine they have to say:

'TREE TASTY. TIGER BAD. WATER COOL. STOMP HUMAN INTO JUNGLE COMPOST.'

Simply, not all language barriers are bad.

That was the case, anyway, during an afternoon spent in the dry sauna that is Tunis with a pair of fellow travelers, only one of who spoke French, the default language for Westerners in Tunisia. The French-speaker, a Boston psychiatrist, told our cabbie he wanted to buy a rug—which is akin to asking a car dealer, 'Do you have anything *more* expensive?'

Apparently, '*ka-ching*' is universal.

We arrived at a magnificent complex of shops, once the home of the regional bey, and were swept efficiently to an upstairs room, where we were welcomed, seated and plied with cardamom-scented tea. The head merchant, who out of pure coincidence turned out to be the cabbie's cousin, launched into his heartfelt welcome, followed by his initial sales pitch—all blessedly in French.

Suddenly, all my worries about endless haggling over carpets I did not need and could not afford disappeared. I simply shrugged my shoulders and smiled sheepishly, avoiding even the French phrase for 'I don't speak French.'

Without the common language, I was no longer a potential buyer. My inability to generate even simple phrases in French—I was equally as likely to converse in elephant—had become my only armor.

The merchant disregarded me as politely as possible and turned back to the Boston shrink (who I think was spoiling for a fight) and the two launched headlong into a match of strategy and wills reminiscent of a Crusade-era siege.

Years later and miles away, I strolled into the Oman mountain village of Al-Hamra, in which every street was a side street and the mud-brick homes seemed at once ancient and temporary. A group of men and boys sitting in front of what could charitably be called a convenience store—the convenience being that you could stand in the middle of the room and still touch every product—beckoned me to sit with them, in Arabic first, then with hand gestures.

I kicked off my flip-flops and sat, feet tucked underneath to avoid cultural faux pas. We took stock of our lingual assets: One teenage boy in the group had maybe thirty words of English; I had seven Arabic phrases. And yet, during the next hour we swapped personal stories, laughed, argued and sang, mostly through gestures, drawings in the dirt, inflection and an embarrassing amount of pantomime (think Marcel Marceau on powerful narcotics).

It was among the best conversations of my life.

I considered the benefits of our language barrier: We had to work harder and earn understanding; nothing was taken for granted; there was no tricky syntax or semantics to misinterpret or that might accidentally offend.

At some point during the hour, a large man driving a Mercedes stopped and delivered a frail-looking gentleman in a lawn chair into the conversation. The older man, once a regional sheikh, according to the boy with thirty words, wore a time-carved scowl as ancient as the mud buildings, but that seemed less flexible.

He spoke few words, none of which I understood. Even if I possessed elephant like infrasonic sound abilities, I'd still be at a loss. But when I stood to leave I tilted my camera to show the sheikh a photo I'd taken of his cranky, craggy expression. He squinted, focused and paused. Then, similar to the changing course of a mighty river, the lines in his face shifted, revealing a broad, improbable grin.

No interpretation was necessary.

★

Spud Hilton is the travel editor of The San Francisco Chronicle, *where since 2000 he has written about, reported on and been hopelessly lost in destinations on six continents. His attempts to divine, describe and defy the expectations of places—from Havana's back alleys to Kyoto's shrines to the floor of a hippie bus in Modesto—have earned six Lowell Thomas Awards, and have appeared in more than sixty newspapers in North America, several of which are still publishing. Spud also writes the Bad Latitude travel blog at SFGate.com and plays cornet in an early New Orleans traditional jazz band.*

Pricier than Prada

There is a high cost to living La Dolce Vita.

For now, I ignore the mail piled in the foyer, take my shoes off, and absorb the warmth of the terra cotta floor. Outside the living room window, a carpet of dandelions welcomes me like a light parade. How I love being in Tuscany in May—the lavender-laced air, hills stretching skyward, birds serenading amidst the hum of tractors.

While straining to keep my eyes open after yesterday's overnight flight from L.A to Rome, I thumb through the mail. On top of the stack, thick with outdated TV guides and newsletters from the village church, is a bill from Siena Ambiente, the garbage company. I rip open the envelope, read the statement twice. What? 581 euros, just for bags. With my head throbbing, I phone Marco, my accountant, for an appointment.

That afternoon, at Marco's office, we exchange the customary, "*Come va?*" and "*Bene, bene.*" Our heels click on the granite as he leads me from the waiting area into his spacious, cantaloupe-colored office.

Once we're seated, Marco says, "The post office was supposed to forward your bill for *rifuiti* here."

"Exactly—this payment was due five months ago." I hand him the statement. "How can a few dozen *sacchetti* cost over 500 euros? That's equivalent to $800."

He idly taps his pen against a marble paperweight. His eyes, a shade darker than his blue shirt, soften, but his words sound like a recording. "The fee is according to the square meters of the house."

"Even for one person?"

"Doesn't matter—ten people in one house would be charged the same. This is Italia." He smiles as if this is as reasonable as ladling tomato sauce over pasta. In a deeper tone, he adds, "Remember, unpaid garbage bills are like tax evasion here."

The thought of being on the *Finanza Guardia's* "Wanted" list sends prickles down my spine.

"Siena Ambiente is only open from 3:00 to 6:00 Mondays and Wednesdays. I suggest you go there now."

During the five-minute drive from Marco's office in Montepulciano's Piazza Grande, down a steep, one-lane road, my foot hovers on the brake pedal. Perspiration drips from my hands as I inch the car around one corkscrew turn after another high above the valley floor.

Once on level ground, I square my shoulders and march through an arched stone entrance into Siena Ambiente's modern headquarters. While waiting in line, a white-haired man rants to the clerk about charges on his statement. How reassuring to hear someone else with "garbage" issues.

After he storms away, shaking his head, I approach the clerk. She peers at my bill and then at me through her Gucci frames. "You must pay in your *Municipio*, Pienza."

"On the statement, this is the address."

"No matter, you cannot pay here."

The next morning, I forsake my usual puttering amongst the roses, now brimming with white and pink buds, and leave for Pienza by nine. My car knows the way by heart. I whip around the first of six hairpin turns, vaguely aware of the cypresses marking the bends in the road. Hopefully I can explain the late payment without subjunctive verbs.

While walking along Pienza's cobblestone thorough-fare, Corso Rosselini, past balconies of flowers and laundry lines flapping from second story windows, a store display catches my eye. I pause. There, among designer purses and scarves, is a pair of open-toe, red leather Prada pumps. The price tag is two hundred euros less than my garbage bill. They are stunning. If only . . . I sigh and push on.

I huff up four stories of the town hall, my sandals thumping against the uneven stone stairs. Upon reaching the bookkeeper's office, the door is locked. In the dimly lit hallway, the hours of operation are posted: Wednesday and Friday, 9:30 to 13:00. I should have known—Italia-today is Tuesday-*chiuso*-closed.

On Wednesday morning, I retrace my route. This time the bookkeeper's door is ajar. A young woman, wedged behind a huge desk in a closet-sized office with a small window overlooking terra cotta rooftops, greets me with a cheerful, "*Buongiorno.*" She scans my bill, checks her computer, and then concludes, "This is not where you pay."

"What do you mean?" I shrug in disbelief. "Why did that clerk send me here?"

"Possibly, she is *incompetente.*" A grin brightens her pale complexion. "The correct office is near the Church of Saint Agnese in Montepulciano." Perhaps sensing my frustration, she adds, "You can pay at the *ufficio postale* in town, but you need cash."

I yank the statement off her desk and leave with a curt, "*Grazie.*" From the town hall, I head to Monte dei Paschi Bank's local branch. Along Corso Rosselini, I wade through throngs of German and American tourists. Any other time, I'd linger and be charmed as they are by structures still vibrant after 500 years.

At the one open bank window, I place the slightly crumpled garbage bill on the counter for the teller to read. "I'd like to transfer funds from my checking account to pay this."

"Please, your ID." I pull my checkbook and passport from my purse. While the teller searches his computer for my account, I glance upward at the bronze crucifix on the wall behind him. If this is a sign assuring comfort or salvation, I'm ready. But once the teller lifts his head and speaks, I realize it's not to be. "That transaction can only be done in Montepulciano, at your home branch."

"Aren't the branches linked by computers?"

"Yes, but I cannot help you." He brushes me aside and motions for the next customer.

What a jerk. I shove the bill, checkbook, and passport into my purse and walk out on the verge of a meltdown.

Dashing back to the car, I'm barraged by scents of baking bread and simmering sauces drifting from windows above the shops along Corso Rosselini. My stomach is growling. As I pass Latte di Luna, a trattoria known for its succulent grilled duck, I almost cave in. But overriding my mounting hunger is reaching Montepulciano before 1:00, when commerce comes to a halt.

At three different points along the winding road from Pienza, men wave red flags for me to stop. I slow. There's no construction. After proceeding a few hundred feet, I'm stopped again. What's going on? The men are wearing chartreuse vests. On the back of their vests, c-r-e-w is emblazoned in bold black letters. That's not Italian. Who are these guys? Why am I the only car out here? In the distance, I spot a man toting a video camera. With my foot glued to the brake, I yell out to the wind. "Come on, for godsake, let's get moving. How can you close the whole road to photograph some poppies?" My hilltop village, a *frazione* or "suburb" of Pienza, provides the backdrop. UNESCO designated this valley a world cultural heritage site. "O.K., it's beautiful, but come on already."

Outside Montepulciano's city walls, a sign reads: production of the Twilight Saga, *New Moon,* until May 30. That explains the guys in chartreuse along the road and the lack of parking here. White tents, generator trucks, trailers, fire engines, police vehicles, and more chartreuse vests cram the municipal parking lot.

While trudging up the road to the bank, the scent of roasting pork wafts overhead. Again, I suppress thoughts of food and quicken my step to reach the bank before the lunchtime closure. The *New Moon* cast and crew have overtaken *centro.* For the filming, large red banners adorn the town portal. Storefronts are veiled behind urns of blood red geraniums. Up ahead, an actress in a hooded blue cape poses below the clock tower.

The repeated chime proclaims half past the hour when I step inside Monti dei Paschi. What a relief to see the teller who usually handles my banking. He calls me to his window. "*Buongiorno, Signora.*" With one hand curled beneath his trimmed beard, he listens to my saga and then nods. "It's true you must pay with cash."

"Can I pay here?"

He clears his throat. "No. You have to pay at GERIT."

My mouth drops open. "What?"

"It's the collection agency for public services." Pointing toward the street, he continues, "Turn left and go about two hundred meters—next to the *Finanza Guardia.*" He counts out five one hundred euro bills and four twenties and lays them on the counter. As I clench the cash, those beguiling red pumps in the Pienza shop window flash before me.

I dart through GERIT's front door at 12:50, ten minutes before closing. There's no one in sight. "*Buongiorno, buongiorno,*" I repeat with increasing volume. Finally a tall blond woman appears at the counter, takes my payment, and gives me a receipt two inches square with faint purple type. For 581 euros, I insist upon a legible document to certify I reached the finish line.

With a bonafide receipt from GERIT tucked in my purse, I stroll back to my car. The street is empty now apart from the production company. As I cross in front of the Church of Saint Agnese, a lanky man strides past, presumably an actor. He is robed in black, his face chalk white, his lids ghoulishly dark, and his lips engorged and red. I find his appearance no more surreal than my eight hundred-dollar garbage bags or this three-day ordeal. It strikes me that the extraordinary is in fact ordinary in Tuscany. That is the reason I stay.

After a twenty-five year career as a clinical psychologist in southern California, Peggy Exton Jaffe followed her bliss and moved to Val d'Orcia in Tuscany, where she has lived part of each year since 1995.

Thank the Good Lord for Duct Tape

Leave the lipstick, take the duct tape.

I AWAKE NAKED IN PRAGUE. I'M ON MY BED BUT THERE ARE NO sheets. The pillowcase is gone. I scramble to my backpack for something to wear, but there's not a stitch of clothing to be found. Confused, I look in my travel-mate's pack, but she too has no clothes.

I vaguely recall giving all my clothes to the hostel's owners for washing the day before.

Trying to assess the situation and retrace my steps, I light my last cigarette from a crushed pack and take a look around. No one is here. Alyssa, my travel mate, is missing and her bed is without sheets as well. I look down from the loft to the sparse, but clean, room below. There are four other beds and, again, the sheets are missing.

My head is pounding. I take a long drag and exhale a plume of dark gray smoke. The familiar comfort of nicotine makes me feel queasy today. I find a sneaker and use its bottom as an impromptu ashtray. I am sitting, without so much as a thong, holding a cigarette butt. Thank God I treated myself to a Brazilian in Paris last week.

Over the pounding, I hear the laughter of Alyssa down the hall. She has a voice that can carry through city blocks—it can make the hairs on the back of your neck stand on end while your whole body tenses in trepidation of her Leo-like need for attention. As irritating as that quality has become throughout many months of travel together, I feel a bit of relief now. If I can follow her voice, perhaps I can learn how I came to be in this *au naturel* state.

With little on hand to cover my naughty bits, I must improvise some coverage if I want to find answers to the multitude of questions whirling about in my mind. There are two pillows within reach and a roll of my trusty silver duct tape in my pack. Taping the two pillows on top of each other lengthwise, I make a short puffy skirt and slip it on. I consider ripping off smaller pieces to make pasties, and cover at least part of my top half, but decide against it: the pain of ripping them off later couldn't possibly be worth it. I descend from the loft via a shaky wooden ladder and catch a glimpse of myself in a mirror: thank the good Lord for duct tape.

My arms wrapped around me, hands firmly cupping my exposed breasts, I make my way down the hallway towards the cluttered and ever-crowded common area. My body feels heavy. My heart thumps with a seemingly irregular beat. My bare feet toddle along a dampened carpet.

Alyssa's voice becomes louder as I approach the paint-chipped doorframe. I hear other, indistinguishable voices around the bend. I take a deep breath and peek around the corner. One by one, each person turns to look in my direction and stops speaking mid-sentence. Dead stares. Pursed lips. Eye rolls. I am openly and collectively judged.

I step into the room and reveal my avant-garde, duct-taped ensemble. The roar of laughter is so piercing that I can't help but throw my hands up over my ears. Jaws drop.

Tits: always a crowd pleaser.

I plop down on a threadbare green sofa and cross my legs. I try to keep a miniscule amount of dignity by not revealing any more of myself than I already have. Still laughing, Alyssa throws me a pillow to cover my top half.

Another backpacker, a good-looking, muscular, twenty-something—who seems oddly familiar—squeezes my shoulders from behind and messes with my hair in a too-affectionate tussle. I am annoyed. He tells me his name is John and asks me how I like my coffee.

"Black," I manage to mutter.

After a good bit of ribbing, and three extra-strength aspirin, my fellow backpackers begin telling my twisted tale.

It all started at Joe's Bar. Right off the Charles Bridge, on the Vltava River, crammed in among Prague's souvenir shops, there is a small non-descript white building with a neon sign flickering in its corner window. This is the home of Joe's Bar: a three-story, happy-hour-loving, back-packer bar.

For the equivalent of loose US change, you could buy one tall, and delightfully cold pilsner of Czech's finest ale and one chilled shot of well vodka. If you wanted to splurge, a shot of absinthe—the green-eyed monster—was all of twice the loose change. Of course I would want to splurge.

I danced. I sang. I played pool. I became friends with a visiting professional soccer team from Bavaria. I lit my nipples on fire—my infamous party trick—for a laugh.

After a couple of hours, I felt the room begin to spin. I left my group and snuck off to the upstairs restaurant. Seated at a corner high-top table, with full view of the restaurant, I ordered cheesy nachos.

The next thing anyone knew, I was on the floor—physically sick with cheese still in the corners of my mouth. The servers were screaming, the fellow patrons thoroughly (and understandably) disgusted, and the police were called. I was immobile and out cold.

Word spread quickly of the drunken young American woman upstairs. Alyssa and my new best friends—the orange-clad Bavarian soccer team—sprang up the stairs to the rescue. My limp, dead-weight body was carried out of the bar and onto the street. Unable to stand, and barely conscious, I was placed face down on the hood of a nearby car while Alyssa and my orange heroes went back into the bar to collect bags and jackets.

The owner of the hood, and the vehicle on which I was most likely drooling, entered the scene. He gently reached around my back, cupped each breast, and lifted my body off his car. He placed me face down on the cobble stone street, then drove away. *Tit's always a crowd pleaser.*

After a long ordeal finding a cab driver willing to take me, we all (minus the soccer team) made it back to the hostel safely. I asked to take a shower.

A fellow hosteller placed me fully clothed and seated upright with knees at my chest, in the corner of the shower stall. He turned on the water, adjusted the temperature, and closed the glass doors behind him. Then, he, along with everyone else, went out on the deck to relax and smoke a thank-you joint, courtesy of my purse.

After a considerable amount of time had elapsed, the same hosteller who had helped me into the shower decided to check on me. He opened the bathroom door and saw that I was unconscious; my heavy wet clothes covering the drain, the water level directly below my lower lip. When he opened the stall, the water rushed out in a wave, flooding the hostel.

The hostellers jumped into high gear, stomping on the sheets, pillowcases and comforters in an attempt to save the saturated carpets. My wet clothes were peeled off of me and thrown on a clothesline to dry. Then my new hero threw me over his shoulder and carried my stripped body up the ladder.

"So who got the show?" I ask.

"That would be me," John says, with a big smile.

By the time the storytelling has ended and my duct tape ensemble, complete with side-boob view, has lost its appeal, the common room has cleared out. John stays behind and pours me another cup of coffee. As the throbbing in my head begins to subside, an overwhelming feeling of shame and remorse for my over-indulgent and destructive actions flood in. I am the reason many people hate Americans.

I hear a clamor in the hall, followed by a gasp; then screaming. I don't understand a single word of Czech.

The hostel owner, a tall, thin middle-aged woman, enters the common room. I sink lower into the couch, clenching the coffee mug as a life preserver. I want to bolt, but I cannot move. I sit there in silence and wait. She pulls on the bottom of her red knit sweater. I hear her sigh heavily and with conviction. She scans the room before speaking.

"Who?"

I lift my hand slowly like a child unsure of the answer.

"How?"

"Absinthe." I answer.

She closes her eyes and lowers her head. She bounces slowly up and down on the balls of her feet.

I stand up, the hair on my arm sticks to a piece of duct tape protruding from my makeshift garb. I have no idea how to translate my regret and embarrassment.

Her eyes lift to mine. I see the glimmer of a smile. Clearly this is not the first time it's happened. And then, she hands me a pile of my freshly laundered clothes.

Even my socks are ironed.

★

Brege Shinn is an East Coast, beach bum, traveling fool, currently squatting (and confused by) the sweltering desert heat of Las Vegas. Her travel philosophy: if you have your passport, your credit card, and a good bit of duct tape, you'll be just fine. Her previous adventures have included trekking in the Kashmiri Himalayas, living in the Costa Rican Rainforest in a tent during the rainy season, and accidentally finding an underground secret entrance to the Louvre in Paris. "Thank the Good Lord for Duct Tape" is her first print publication. She hopes excessive celebrating for this honor won't result in a repeat performance.

Acknowledgments

Maggi Pecora for helping me when I needed it most. Thank you for your love, wisdom, and your critical eye, and for saving me from alien abduction in Coconut Grove.

Natalie Baszile for her dedication and superior multitasking abilities. I am indebted to you always. I owe you a fine bottle of wine. Heck, I owe you an entire wine bar!

Kimberly Nelson Coombs for her design sensibility and willingness to collaborate on such a fun cover.

James O'Reilly & Larry Habegger—The dynamic duo of travel publishing. You two are God's gift to travel writing and especially for women's travel writing. Thank you so much for this opportunity.

Sean O'Reilly for the completely ludicrous email exchanges, Lady Iguana sends out a tip 'o the hat and a flip of the tail, in a platonic lizard like way.

Jen Leo for trailblazing the way forward with *Sand in My Bra*.

Stephanie Elizondo Griest for her experienced advice and friendship.

Lily Chou for her late night phone calls of encouragement, travel escapades and appetite for adventure.

And for Roger who provides everything under the sun that makes my life meaningful.

"Drug Money" by Katie Eigel published with permission from the author. Copyright © 2012 by Katie Eigel.

"Karma at the Colombo Airport" by Jessica Langlois published with permission from the author. Copyright © 2012 by Jessica Langlois.

"Hollywood Fiction" by Troy Rodrigues published with permission from the author. Copyright © 2012 by Troy Rodrigues.

"Naked, with A Passport" by Allison J. Stein first appeared on *World Hum*, June 2010. published with permission from the author. Copyright © 2010 by Allison J. Stein.

"The Nakuru Scam" by Sylvie Downes published with permission from the author. Copyright © 2012 by Sylvie Downes.

"Embedded in the Boot" by Jennifer Massoni published with permission from the author. Copyright © 2012 by Jennifer Massoni.

"Advice for Closet Cougars" by Jill Paris published with permission from the author. Copyright © 2012 by Jill Paris.

"Mt. Fuji in a Trash Bag" by Sarah Katin published with permission from the author. Copyright © 2012 by Sarah Katin.

"Flashed in Fallouja" by Kelly Hayes-Raitt published with permission from the author. Copyright © 2012 by Kelly Hayes-Raitt.

"Ditching Fist Impressions" by Kimberley Lovato published with permission from the author. Copyright © 2012 by Kimberley Lovato.

"Safari Sickness" by Julian Worker published with permission from the author. Copyright © 2012 by Julian Worker.

"Meeting Mosquito" by Josey Miller published with permission from the author. Copyright © 2012 by Josey Miller.

"Wasted in Margaritaville" by Jill K. Robinson published with permission of the author. Copyright © 2012 by Jill K. Robinson.

"Cabin Pressure" by Diane Letulle published with permission from the author. Copyright 2012 by Diane Letulle.

"Sometimes a Language Barrier Isn't" by Spud Hilton was originally published in the *San Francisco Chronicle*, October 25, 2009. Published with permission from the author. Copyright © 2009 by Spud Hilton.

"Pricier Than Prada" by Peggy Exton Jaffe published with permission from the author. Copyright © 2012 by Peggy Exton Jaffe.

"Thank the Good Lord for Duct Tape" by Brege Shinn published with permission from the author. Copyright © 2012 by Brege Shinn.

About the Editor

Marcy Gordon has laughed her way through 27 countries, many of them before the age of fourteen in the company of her travel-writing mother. She lived in Italy and worked for The Touring Club of Italy, as contributing editor and co-designer of the Authentic Italy guidebook series. Her narrative writing has been featured on-line and in print in many Travelers' Tales anthologies including *Best Women's Travel Writing 2010 & 2011*, *More Sand in My Bra*, *30 Days in Italy*, and *The Thong Also Rises*. She writes a popular blog about wine and wine tourism called Come for the Wine (www.comeforthewine.com) and is the founder of Writing Between the Vines—Vineyard Retreats for Writers, an artist–in–residence program on vineyard estates around the world (www.writingbetweenthevines.org). She is a graduate of the University of Florida, College of Journalism and Communications.